Elite Dating Secrets: How the Top 1% of Men Meet, Attract, and Date Beautiful Women

By Jon Anthony

Legality

Table of Contents

Acknowledgements...5

Author's Note..6

Introduction...7

Part 1: Unplugging..12

    Chapter 1. Why You Should Listen to Me............15

    Chapter 2. The 6 Core Red Pill Tenets...................21

    Chapter 3. The 5 Stages of Red Pill.....................35

Part 2: What Women Want.......................................40

    Chapter 4. Why You Should Never Trust
Women For Dating Advice.......................................42

    Chapter 5. Short Term vs. Long Term
Attraction Triggers...44

    Chapter 6: Becoming The Alpha Male..................49

    Chapter 7: Alpha Male Personality Traits............51

    Chapter 8: Alpha Male Appearance.....................66

Part 3: Game...89

    Chapter 9. What is Game?...............................92

    Chapter 10. Types of Game.............................95

Part 4: Meeting Women..113

    Chapter 11. Where to Meet Women.....................116

    Chapter 12. How to Meet Women.......................133

    Chapter 13. How to Know if She's Interested......148

    Chapter 14. Doing The Numbers.......................154

Part 5: Dating Girls...156

    Chapter 15. Acing The First Date......................159

    Chapter 16. Location, Location, Location...........161

    Chapter 17. Second Date and Beyond................164

Part 6: Plate Spinning..167

    Chapter 18. What is Plate Spinning? 170

    Chapter 19. The Iron Rule of Harems................172

Chapter 20. How to Build A Harem......................176
Part 7: How Women Should Fit into Your Life.................184
Chapter 21. Defining Your Goal............................187
Chapter 22. Finding Your Ideal Woman...............189
Chapter 23. Screening Women...........................191
Part 8: The Iron Rules of Jon..195
Final Thoughts...234

Acknowledgements

I would like to thank my mother, for teaching me to love others, with a kind and gentle heart, no matter what they've done to you, or what they've become. I would like to thank my sister, for teaching me to be a protector – to be patient when times are hard, and to give people space when they're going through change in their lives. I would like to thank my father for teaching me discipline; for teaching me that to do a job well done, is the only way to do a job.

I would like to thank my mentors, both in-person, and those who I've never met. I would like to thank Tony Robbins, for dedicating his life to helping others change theirs. I would like to thank Dr. Robert Anton Wilson, for opening my eyes to how the human mind works. I would like to thank Dr. David Hawkins, for teaching me to let go, and Eckhart Tolle, for teaching me to be present.

I would like to thank all of the women in my life, who have taught me many lessons – some of which were very difficult to learn, and some of which were not learned easily. Throughout your life, you will find that women will test you, over and over again, until you finally learn the lesson that you need to understand. I thank them for this.

I would also like to express my gratitude to you, the reader, for picking up this book. You are embarking on a journey that will not only transform your dating life, but that will have long-lasting ramifications for your entire life as a whole. You may not realize it yet, but the ideas and secrets hidden within this book, will not just allow you to date beautiful women, but when applied to your life in full, they will also transform your income, health, and happiness.

Author's Note

Dear reader... thank you for purchasing this book! It's filled with everything I have learned about women over the past several years. I have no doubt that if you apply the advice contained within this book, you will be dating more women than you know what to do with, in no time.

This book is meant to be a helpful companion; one that you will return to over the years, when you are struggling with a particular woman, or with women as a whole.

If you enjoy this book and would like to purchase my premium video courses and programs, you can do by heading to: Masculinedevelopment.com/Products

If you would like to download the kindle edition of this eBook, which contains relevant, in-context links to various articles on my website, please shoot me an email, and I will send you a copy for free, as a gift to you.

I am always free to answer reader questions, so if you have any questions about women, dating, or life in general, you can send me an email here, and I will do my best to get back to you: jon@masculinedevelopment.com

All in all, I hope you thoroughly enjoy this eBook. The journey you will make will be a long and difficult one at times, but it is so, so worth it.

Introduction

"When the student is ready, the master will appear." -Three Initiates, *The Kybalion*

"They journey of a thousand miles, begins with a single step." -Lao Tzu

Why This Book Matters

As I'm sitting here, writing this book, I'm struggling to convey just how vital this new and emerging world of masculine advice is. As I've been writing, blogging, and producing content over the past several years, all of my experience has confirmed our need for a change.

Over the past three years, I've encountered thousands of men who are lost. Men who have had their hearts broken from a terrible relationship and men who have almost killed themselves due to such a deep sense of depression and ostracization. The men in our culture are lost, and we are desperately searching for a new way of life.

We have forgotten the way of the past; the way of men. We've forgotten how to lead meaningful and fulfilling lives, how to approach our work lives, how to stand up for what we believe in, and how to deal with the opposite sex.

I deal with men who are angry, bitter, and cynical towards women on a day-to-day basis. I empathize with their pain, and I understand that the dating sphere has changed drastically over the past several generations – so much so that your Grandparents will find it impossible to relate to some of the problems that men deal with today.

Flakiness, dishonesty, and outright manipulation are some of the problems that modern men face when dating modern women. I want to make it clear that I love women. I love sleeping with women, I love dating women, and I love being with women. But to deny the harsh reality that we face in today's world is unacceptable. Women have changed, or rather, many of the social and cultural pressures that encouraged traditional relationships, have changed.

This book is an honest attempt to fight this, by arming men with the knowledge they need to effectively face the dating world today. Many men are approaching dating in the current year, using a map handed down from their Grandparents – and while that map may have worked in the 1950s, it is pathetically ineffective today.

To all of the men facing problems with women today, I empathize with your story. As you'll soon learn, I was not born with "natural game," as they call it. In fact, I was incredibly inept with women for most of my early childhood and teens. It wasn't until I stumbled upon the secrets that you will discover in this book, that my life began to change forever.

Using the secrets that I will share with you in this book, I've effectively seduced and dated some of the most stunning women I've ever met. I've slept with well over 100 women in the past few years alone, and I've forged relationships with some of them that will likely last a lifetime.

The truth is out there, and the truth is in here – you simply must be ready to use it. If you had handed me this book during my early teenage years, I would have never even read it. Even if I had, I would likely have rejected it out of complete denial or anger.

Many of the facts contained in this book will be offensive to many, but if you can accept them, move on, and integrate them into your life, then a future in the top 1% of men awaits you.

How to Read This Book

This book should be treated more as a helpful companion than as some boring text to be read once and never touched again. Much of the advice in this book will not seem accurate, useful, or relevant, until you are ready to receive it.

There have been times in my life where I watched a video, purchased a course, or read an eBook, and thought nothing of it, only to revisit it several years later and wonder how in the hell I couldn't see the deep, life-changing knowledge found within it. This may be the case for you, with Elite Dating Secrets.

I recommend that you read this book from start to finish the very first time. This will give you a good overview and understanding of many of the tactics, techniques, and belief systems that I use in my own dating life, and that all successful men use in their dating lives as well. From here, you are welcome to return to it any time you wish and consult its guidance.

If you are having a problem with a particular woman, consider skipping ahead to whichever part you believe is most pertinent. As I said, I recommend you treat this book as a helpful companion first and foremost, which should be consulted on numerous occasions.

If you are picking this book up, and want to start meeting, attracting, and dating beautiful women as fast as possible, then skip ahead and read Part 2, Part 4, and Part 8. Part 2 will explain what women want, Part 4 will provide you with the mechanics of meeting women, and Part 8 will give you a distinct set of "Iron Rules" to always follow with women.

For your convenience, I have placed an "Executive Summary" before each part of this book. This is for you to gain an idea of what each part is about, and to quickly and easily grasp the core concepts that each part discusses. Do not forego reading this book altogether, just for the executive summaries, but still – I believe they are useful as an "introduction" to each part.

It takes time for your "old self" to die off, and for your "new self" to be created, which is why you must constantly reinforce your "new self" with knowledge from seminars, books, tapes, and more. The old, blue pilled self is reluctant to die off, and the new, red pilled self is slow to be created.

With this in mind, my friend, I genuinely hope that this book changes your life. I've probably never met you, although you may have left a comment on my blog at one point, and I may have responded. Perhaps you're one of the few who I've coached over the years, or maybe you and I have sent each other numerous emails. Regardless, I thank you for picking up this book.

Your dating life is your journey, and the path you take is entirely up to you – but never forget to continually return to this book, as a guide in times when you need it most.

Part 1: Unplugging

"This is your last chance. After this, there is no turning back. You take the blue pill - the story ends, you wake up in your bed and believe whatever you want to believe. You take the red pill - you stay in Wonderland and I show you how deep the rabbit-hole goes."

-Morpheus, *The Matrix*

"So entrapped are we in our self-expectation and self-imposed limitations that we fail to see that we have always had the keys to our own prisons - we're just scared shitless to use them."

-Rollo Tomassi, *The Rational Male*

Executive Summary

In short, most men are entirely brainwashed into having certain beliefs which make them fail miserably with attracting the opposite sex. This set of beliefs, which repulse women, are collectively known as "The Blue Pill," taken from the Matrix. "The Red Pill," on the other hand, signifies the set of beliefs which are *reality-based*, and not just based on fairytales.

After discovering the "red pill," most men go through five distinct phases, similar to the Kübler-Ross model, starting off with denial, and finally ending with acceptance. Throughout this book, you will be exposed to many red pill beliefs, which may cause you to grow angry. Do not give in to your emotions, as tempting as it may be. Accept these facts for what they are: facts.

Fundamentally, women are hypergamous by nature. This is why 20% of men get 80% of the women. Women are highly emotional and make most decisions based on how they feel. This is contrary to men, who are more logical, and make most decisions based on what they think.

Women will sometimes settle down with a man who has money, but crave the love of an alpha male. When you're trying to attract women, never lead with money. Always lead with confidence, assertiveness, dominance, and decisiveness.

Women love sex just as much as men, even though they will never admit it. They love assholes, because assholes say what they think, and do what they want. Women hate nice guys, because they are fundamentally manipulative. They believe that being nice to a woman obligates her to return sex. Unfortunately, true attraction cannot be negotiated.

There is no "oneitis," or "the one." These are fairytale imaginings that may feel warm and fuzzy on the inside, but in reality, prevent you from experiencing true abundance with women. If you wish to experience this abundance, and have your choice of mates, you must "swallow the red pill" and accept the difficult-to-accept concepts discussed throughout this book.

Chapter 1: Why You Should Listen to Me

As I'm writing this right now, I've actually got 4 separate girls vying for my attention for which one I see tonight. They're all college students, the youngest being 19 and the oldest being 23, which is typically the age range I date within (I'm 24). I say this not to brag, but to show you just how far I've come.

This was not at all how it's always been; in fact, most of my life was characterized by being a severe incel with some deep-rooted beta male beliefs. I like to believe I was born a natural alpha male, but circumstances somehow made me forget my biology, and buy into the modern feminized belief systems which so viciously destroy many men's lives.

I was born to a pretty regular middle-class family. My parents both got married when they were in their late 20's, and about a year later I came along. I distinctly remember being in Kindergarten and "kissing tongues" with a girl named Diana, who apparently had a pretty big crush on the 5-year-old me. Oh, how the times were good.

It wasn't long however, until my natural state of being was changed. After a slew of incidents that happened when I was around the age of 7, I ended up having a nervous breakdown to the point of being hospitalized. The doctors thought it was a "brain tumor," but I later found out that it was merely due to severe psychological trauma.

Regardless, it left me quite socially isolated. I became that "weird kid," who had terrible ADHD and OCD; that kid who the teachers hated dealing with. I used to wash my hands repeatedly, sometimes over 100 times, before I "got it right."

I would spend hours re-writing my homework, because I was furious that it wasn't perfect. Every single word, every single letter, every single dashed "T" and dotted "i" had to be absolutely pristine; otherwise I'd have to redo the entire assignment.

Now, of course, I know what you're thinking. I must've gotten all the babes with such a severe psychological disorder, right? Well, funny enough I actually did manage to get a few girls into me come middle school (after I overcame the OCD), but they never ended up leading to any sort of dates. I could tell they were interested in me, but I just never knew what to do.

I spent most of my middle school years as a recluse, retreating to my basement and playing videogames like World of Warcraft, Halo 3, and RuneScape. I would spend hours playing those games just to avoid socializing, and of course, it only made my problems worse. There was a brief respite however, which came when I was 14. I've mentioned it a few times on my blog and during my podcast but have never told the full story.

In short, I somehow managed to meet a girl at the pool near my house, and she was a complete nymphomaniac. She asked for my number, told me that she wanted to have sex, and of course, my 14-year-old self was ecstatic. So, we met up one day, and she confidently led the way – she knew what she wanted and wasn't afraid to tell me.

We wound up having sex in a forest nearby the pool, but I never came inside of her, so I don't know if that technically counts as losing your virginity, though.

In fact, it wasn't until 7 years later (when I turned 21), that I was able to cum inside of a girl for the first time. We'll get there in a second, but back to middle school – I was bullied pretty roughly, so whatever feelings of confidence I had from banging Michaela (that was her name) were totally eradicated.

Every day I was confronted with bullying and rejection, to the point that I became almost a complete social recluse. I had very few friends, and the ones I did have weren't real friends. Eventually, I had enough – and that's where my awakening began.

Discovering the Red Pill

As I began to grow tired of mindlessly grinding my World of Warcraft character to level 70, my interests began to shift onto something else entirely: social status. For whatever reason, I became utterly fascinated with why some kids were cool, and some weren't.

Around the age of 14, I discovered the manosphere. In retrospect, this was my saving grace. Had I not found the wisdom of Roosh from Return of Kings, the writings of Rollo from The Rational Male, and the dozens of other eBooks, PDF's, and "free reports" that I read, I don't know if I'd even be here writing this now.

Regardless, I began to delve into the world of the manosphere. It struck me as uniquely simple and easy to understand, compared to most of the modern dating advice that you've probably read on websites like "Men's Health" and "Your Tango." For the record – and you can absolutely quote me on this – 99% of mainstream dating advice is absolute garbage. This book is the antidote. This book is the cure. But I digress...

As I discovered the manosphere, I slowly began to implement its advice into my life. At first, it was simple things, like mastering eye contact, learning alpha male body language, and other "surface level" hacks. Over time however, I began to change as a person.

I got my first "real" girlfriend when I turned 18 – her name was Sophia. She was a beautiful Cuban girl who was about an inch taller than me, and for whatever reason, she was obsessed with me. In fact, she actually initiated most of the interactions we had.

She asked for my number before I asked for hers. She invited me over to her house before I ever had to make a move. She even gave me a blowjob, without me having to ask. All because of the mindset shifts and techniques I'm going to teach you in this book.

Fast forward a year, and I was off to college. Ah, finally! A chance to put my "forbidden knowledge" of pickup artistry to work. Finally, I had a whole dormitory to myself (and a roommate of course, but that was better than my parents). Unfortunately, my ambitions were quickly halted after I wound up severely injuring my left hand.

For my entire first semester, I stayed in, not going to a single party. Still though, I spent this time wisely – I browsed PUA forums, scoured the manosphere for wisdom, and even bought a few products along the way. Eventually, once my injury healed, I was free to go.

The next few years was quite the wild ride. Every chance I got, I was trying to enhance my skills. Getting girls' numbers from classes, going out to frat parties, and meeting women on Tinder.

I spent years perfecting online dating, split-testing profiles, experimenting with openers, flow charts, and sequences, and playing with different profile bios. Eventually, I got it down to a science, and set my sights on cold approaching.

For quite some time, there wasn't a night that I didn't go out. I'd approach girls at the gym, I'd approach girls on the streets, I'd even approach nurses in the doctor's office. I was obsessed with this newfound power called "game," and I wanted to master it.

Eventually, I started "Masculine Development," my blog which has over 250 free articles on dating advice, health and fitness, making money, and more. Now, at the age of 24, I'm fully self-employed, earning $15,000/month (and growing). I love what I do, and I do what I love.

I teach guys to get chicks for a living – how the hell did that happen again? Well, it wasn't without some blood, sweat, and tears along the way, but somehow my dreams came true. I'm writing this book not so much out of necessity, but out of a genuine desire to help you.

I want to see you succeed. I want you to date your dream girl. I want you to have the life that you've always dreamed of, and I want you to achieve it with my help. Before we get there though, I need to uncover some of the biggest myths of the manosphere, which left unaddressed, can potentially ruin your life many times over.

Dispelling Truth from Falsehood

I'm ashamed to admit this, but when I first discovered the manosphere, I was primarily motivated by anger. I'm sure many of you can relate to this – as it's hard not to be angry sometimes. When you've been taught your whole life that "being a nice guy" is the way to get girls, and then it blows up in your face and ends with constant rejection, it's kind of hard not to get resentful.

Over the years though, I learned to let go of my anger. As I grew as a person, I started to understand the importance of not judging reality, but merely accepting it for what it is. I stopped getting angry at girls for wanting attention and, well... acting like girls.

I've come to accept female sexuality for what it is, and in fact, I rather enjoy it. Unfortunately, however, many writers on the manosphere have not yet reached this place. Many writers on the manosphere are still filled with hatred and anger towards women, and thus their work is tainted with such sentiment.

It is essential to understand that a considerable portion of the "manosphere" is written by incels. And I'm not discounting the work of guys such as Donovan Sharpe, Roosh, Rollo, or Roissy, either – I'm simply telling things how they are.

In fact, I once had a conversation with a VERY prominent manosphere writer (whose name I will not divulge), and he said these exact words to me: "Jon, I'm ashamed to admit it, but I'm still a virgin." This was a guy who was writing articles daily on how to get girls.

I don't say this to discourage you from reading everything you can and learning everything you must, but rather to give you realistic expectations. Throughout this book, I will debunk common manosphere myths and give you the "real deal" without any emotional investment whatsoever.

I would also like to point out that, as a whole, the manosphere has helped men. Period. It has saved countless men from the pitfalls of divorce, and it's made many men's' lives far better. It's not perfect, but it's still a force for good. Understand that not all advice is accurate, and it's often hard to parse truth from falsehood. That being said, let's get into some truth.

Chapter 2: The 6 Core Red Pill Tenets

I would like to start the book off with a very powerful set of tenets – a collection of statements that are inherently "red pill," and that you must work to internalize. These statements will not be easy to swallow. In fact, many of them will be outright infuriating to hear, just because they go against the grain of a very gynocentric and feminized society.

From the time you were born, you've been taught to buy into the "Matrix." You've been conditioned and brainwashed, to accept a specific set of beliefs, that whether you realize it or not, are harming you with women, and with life as a whole.

With this in mind, I've created a set of six "Red Pill Tenets" that serves as an excellent introduction to the manosphere, and to the red pill as a whole. Here they are.

1. Women Are Hypergamous By Nature

The term "hypergamy" was infamously coined by Rollo Tomassi, and he has gone to incredible lengths to describe this phenomenon. In short, "hypergamy" refers to a woman's natural inclination to date up, as far as she can, to get the best possible mate for herself.

Now, I know what you're thinking. That seems obvious, doesn't it? Of course, women want to get the best possible mate. Don't men want the hottest girlfriend they can get, too?

Yes, but it isn't that simple. When we look across large groups of people, we see some very distinct trends, that are on one hand unsettling, but on the other hand, liberating.

Take a look at the image below, for example, which illustrates the dating patterns of men and women on a large scale.

HYPERGAMY

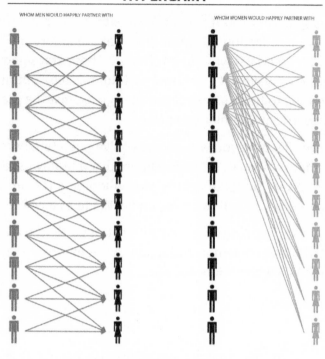

As you can see, men will often times happily partner with a girl who is understood to be "at his level" or even slightly below his level. Men are generally far less picky at choosing mates, for many reasons which will be discussed throughout this book.

Women, on the other hand, are far pickier when it comes to selecting mates. All across cultures, regardless of time and geographical distance, we find that women tend to marry up. What this means is that they prefer men who are "out of their league."

To simplify the dating world, we have created a concept known as "Sexual Marketplace Value," or "SMV" for short. This is simply the objective sexual value of a person, or in other words, how attractive this person is seen to the opposite sex.

Take, for example, a man like Channing Tatum. Do you think he has a low SMV? Of course not. Millions of girls dream about marrying Channing Tatum, for many reasons. Thus, his sexual marketplace value is exceptionally high, and he's seen to be at the top of the totem pole.

Now compare Channing Tatum, to let's say, Danny DeVito. How high do you think good old Danny's sexual marketplace value is? Not very high, of course. While plenty of women fantasize about meeting Channing Tatum one day, not many fantasize about meeting Danny DeVito.

Thankfully, you're lucky as a man, because you can increase your SMV over time. A man's "sexual marketplace value" is determined by many factors, which we will discuss throughout this book, but the most crucial point to take away is this: women date up and across, men date across and down.

Understanding this simple concept explains so much of female behavior. Here are some examples of how female hypergamy affects your life:

- It's why all the girls seem to flock to a handful of guys
- It's why getting out of the bottom 50% of men can be so hard
- It's why women routinely divorce men, when they realize they have better options
- It's why women will fuck the celebrity (up) and marry the stable guy (across)

It's also why dating for men gets harder and harder, as women get more and more financial and political power in a country.

Previously, in the mid-1850's, any guy who had a stable income was considered "above" her, and deemed worthy of dating.

Now? Most girls have college degrees and jobs that earn $60k/year. To be considered a "catch" nowadays, you have to be earning at least 6 figures, and probably very good looking, too. In liberating themselves, women have unwittingly shrunk their dating pool, which unfortunately is why we're starting to see many more women in their 30's and 40's without a husband to be with.

Female hypergamy also explains why 1% of guys get to date 99% of girls. Every single girl in the world wants to be fucked by a rockstar, a celebrity, an actor, a millionaire, or a "fuckboy." They will never admit it publicly, and some won't even admit it to themselves – but it's 100% true.

Most men grow angry when faced with the concept of hypergamy. "B-but she should love me for who I am!" he'll exclaim. Of course. So, if your girlfriend grew 300 pounds overweight, but still had the same "great personality," would you still "love her for who she is?" Of course not. You might enjoy her personality, but obviously, you wouldn't be attracted to her anymore.

I'm not saying that love doesn't exist, either – it clearly does. I'm simply pointing out the fact that women are hypergamous by nature. They all prefer to marry up, and will hardly ever "settle" unless they are absolutely forced to (more on "The Wall" later).

In short, the "bad news" is that if you're in the bottom 50% of men, you will likely not get any female interest. The "good news" is that with some effort, although it may take time, you can easily catapult yourself to the top 10% or even 1%, and have a wide range of dating options.

2. Women Are Highly Emotional

Again, this may seem extremely obvious, but it absolutely boggles my mind that most men don't understand this simple phenomenon. Anyone with half a brain knows that women are more emotional than men – this is due to millions of years of evolutionary biology.

Yes, women are still capable of rational thought, just as men are still capable of emotions. I'm not saying that women operate 100% on feelings. If I had to give it a percentage, I'd say that they run 70% on emotions, and 30% on logic, whereas men are the other way around.

Let's take a look at the work of Dr. Louann Brizendine, for example. She wrote a book entitled "The Female Brain," in which she accurately describes many of the distinct differences between how men and women think. I highly recommend you read it, because it will shed some light on why women seem so "crazy" to men, when in reality, they're just emotional.

> *"Males have double the brain space and processing power devoted to sex as females. Just as women have an eight-lane superhighway for processing emotion while men have a small country road, men have O'Hare airport as a hub for processing thoughts about sex whereas women have the airfield nearby that land for small and private planes."*

Understanding these simple differences between men and women can shed light on so many relationship problems that take place in the modern world. When you fully internalize how emotions-oriented women are, not only will you gain an appreciation for them as women, but you will understand them more fully.

Just this simple concept alone explains so much of female behavior. Here are some "examples" of how female emotionality affects your life:

- It's why women sleep with the men who can make them FEEL things, even if those men aren't "logically" the best option for them
- It's why women will consistently date the "asshole" or "player" even though it doesn't make logical sense: because he can make her FEEL things other guys can't
- It's why women will frequently say one thing, then do another. They're not lying per se, but rather, as their emotions change, so do their decisions.
- It's why they make better caretakers than men do. They're more "in tune" with what children are feeling, due to more finely-tuned social circuits in their brains
- It's why even "good girls" will become "sluts" in highly emotionally charged environments such as spring break, rock concerts, or crazy parties.

Understanding that women are emotional creatures first and logical creatures second, is one of the most important things you can get into your head. When you fully internalize that the master pickup artist makes her FEEL, rather than makes her THINK, you will understand women and game.

3. Alpha Fucks vs. Beta Bucks

Feeding off of the hypergamy concept, we will go even deeper. Women's biology is torn between two intersecting, but often competing, needs:

1. To get the best genes possible
2. To secure a stable provider male

This is where the dichotomy of "alpha fucks and beta bucks" comes from. This is also sometimes called the "lover vs. provider" distinction. In short, it simply means that women tend to categorize men into two different categories – lovers and providers.

The "lovers" are the men who are sexy. They're the men who have great genes, are physically fit, have good game, and are fun above all else. They're the type of guy every man wants to become – because they get more ass than a public toilet seat.

Then, there are the "providers." These are the men who women aren't necessarily attracted to, but who they deem would be loyal and reliable partners. These are the lawyers and doctors, who a woman might marry, but won't necessarily want for a one-night stand.

Now, here's the critical part – ideally, women want BOTH of these traits in a man. They want the confident, funny, charismatic, and sexy alpha male (the lover), and they want him to be WILLING to stick around and provide for her.

But, because alpha males often have so many options with women, they're hard to secure. Only the most beautiful models and actresses can secure a Leonardo DiCaprio or a Brad Pitt for marriage – and even then, once she gets older and her looks fade, he might not stick around.

Do you see the catch? The "alpha males" with the best genes are desperately wanted by women, but they hardly ever stick around. So, what's a girl to do? Some women "settle" for a provider male. Others fuck the alpha, and lie to the provider, telling him that it's his child.

Hence, women evolved the "alpha fucks vs. beta bucks" filter. They quickly and accurately put men into one of these two categories. Much of what I teach you in this book will simply be

27

meant to take you OUT of the "provider" category and put you into the "lover" category.

Let me tell you something to illustrate this concept very clearly...

Whenever I go out, I rarely talk about work. In fact, when girls ask me what I do for a living, 99% of the time I say I'm a drug dealer and do porn.

Why? It's simple – the second a girl realizes you have MONEY, she realizes that you can be a provider for her. She slots you into the "beta bucks" category, and because of that, will typically make you wait for a few dates before she fucks you.

I know this will be a complete mindfuck to most guys, but it's 100% true. I know guys who have huge $10 million-dollar mansions, and they seldom bring girls back there before they've fucked them. Why? Again, it's beta bucks, alpha fucks.

The girls will be completely DTF, but the second they see he has a $10 million mansion, suddenly they change their approach. On a subconscious level, women think: "Wait a minute... this guy has money. What if I make him take me on a few dates before I fuck him?"

This is why traveling across Europe in hostels will ALWAYS get you laid more than living in a $10 million mansion. There's never a question of you being a "provider," because she doesn't see that you make a ton of money.

Here are some examples of "alpha fucks vs. beta bucks" at play:

- It's why women will fuck rockstars and celebrities, then marry some chump
- It's why women fuck drug dealers, club promoters, and other broke guys, but then make rich dentists, lawyers, and doctors shell out for a peck on the cheek

28

- It's why 1% of guys fuck 99% of girls – because they're the "alpha fucks"

Now – does this mean you shouldn't strive to make money? Of course not. I actively tell my students to start businesses on the side, and I actively COACH them to do so. What's important is that you make money for you, not for girls.

As a side note as well, having more money CAN get you laid more... but only if you use it properly. Most guys think buying a Rolex, a Mercedes Benz, and living in a mansion will get them laid all of the time. Funny enough, it usually backfires. In fact, it usually gets them slotted as a beta orbiter, rather than a "lover."

Do you know what would get them laid WAY more? Spending that $10 million on a small apartment in Las Vegas, with a hot tub, a ton of cocaine, and installing a stripper pole in their house. Logistics, fun, and "alpha fucks" will always trump money.

This is why I never take girls on expensive dates until we've been dating and fucking for months. The first date is always coffee (remember this). Make her screen herself. See if YOU like HER, not the other way around. If she passes your criteria, then take her on a second date, which is meant to spike her emotions. I'll talk more about this in Part 5.

4. Women Love Sex Just As Much As Men

One of the BIGGEST myths out there is that women don't want to fuck. This is complete bullshit, and I'm speaking from personal experience in banging over 150 women. Women want to fuck _just as much as men do._ In fact, sometimes they want to fuck even more.

The thing is though, you have to be the "right guy." Do women want to fuck the average guy's brains out? Of course not. But if you have tight game, and employ the strategies discussed throughout this book? They will be desperate to fuck you.

The standard retort to this claim is that it's biologically impossible for women to be as horny as men, because they don't have as much testosterone as we do. While this is true, it doesn't take into account a massive reason that women fuck men – for their validation and attention.

Let me tell you a story about a girl I met when I was in college...

I met this girl, let's call her "Jennifer," in one of my classes. We immediately hit it off, and I got her number. Throughout the semester, she would vie for my attention, but because I knew enough game to make her work for it, she grew increasingly sexually frustrated.

It got to the point that she would talk about the anatomy of the penis, and how she was "learning" it for one of her med school classes. She would talk about how she knew all the pleasure points on the penis, and how she gave incredible blowjobs.

Yet, I stayed true to my PUA tactics. I would give her small doses of validation, complimenting her, and/or giving her attention, in exchange for a lot of work on her end. Eventually, she got fed up and invited me over to her house one night.

All of her friends were there, and we were all pre-gaming for the night. Right as we were about to leave, she said that she "wasn't feeling good" and wanted me to stay back and watch her. Of course, I saw the look on her female friends' faces – they all knew what was really going on. She wanted to be alone with me. They understood this and went on their way.

The second that her friends left the house, she literally grabbed my hands, and PULLED – and I mean with all her might – she PULLED me into her bedroom, and onto her bed. She jumped on top of me, took her shirt off, and started making out with me. We proceeded to fuck like monkeys for the next three hours.

Now, I know what you're thinking. "Okay, that's one girl... but isn't that the exception to the rule?" Thankfully, it's not. Most girls out there love having sex... it just has to be with the right man. You have to know how to turn her on, and how to get her chasing you, both of which we will talk about throughout this book.

I've had girls tell me that they haven't had sex in three months – and I can tell that they're not lying. But for some reason, when they meet me, they start texting me every week to fuck. My life literally looks like a porno at times, with the things girls beg me to do to them. I'm not saying this to brag, I'm saying it so that you know what's possible.

The key takeaway is that girls LOVE to fuck... IF, and this is the big IF, you're the right guy.

5. Women Like "Assholes"

Have you ever heard the phrase that women love assholes? Well, it's sort of true, but not entirely true. The reason I put "assholes" in parenthesis is because on some level, women do like assholes.

They like the cockiness that assholes exude. They love the chase of fighting for his validation. They love a man who's on his purpose, whose attention is rare. They love a man who plays hard to get, and who can make her feel excitement.

31

This doesn't mean to be emotionally or physically abusive, at all. This is not what I mean by being an asshole. In my article, "How to Be An Asshole Women Want," I summed it up perfectly:

> *"It isn't necessarily assholes that women like. It's strong men who can <u>sometimes</u> act like assholes. That's the key difference here. It's not enough to just be an asshole all the time. You have to learn how to be an asshole <u>in the right way.</u>"*

In other words, women are attracted to men who have the potential to be assholes. Why is this? Let's take a quick look at evolutionary biology.

Most of our history was pretty rough. At any moment, a neighboring tribe could slaughter half of your village, and rape all of the women in sight. Wild animals could kill you during the night, your family and friends could die of starvation, or freeze to death during the winter.

Women evolved to want strong men, because they were the only men who made it through these times alive. When a man acts like an asshole in response to "inappropriate" behavior, such as her bitching at him, disrespecting him, or playing games with him, it shows that he's in control of his own destiny, and that he's a strong man who has a spine.

In short, this is why women love assholes. In a world of weak, pandering white knights and beta male cucks, when a man is an asshole, he sends a message to women loud and clear: "I'm not afraid to stand up for my boundaries and needs, and if you fuck me, I will give you a strong alpha male son who is not afraid to do the same, either."

6. There Is No "Oneitis"

I hate to break it to you, but there is no such thing as "the one." There might be girls that you decide to date for a long time, and there might be a girl you decide to "settle down with," but don't ever fool yourself into thinking that there's only "one girl" for you.

The fact of the matter is that there are 3.5 billion girls in the world, soon to be even more, and as much as it might hurt to admit that your "oneitis" is anything but, it's actually quite liberating.

Now, I'm not saying that you can't fall deeply in love with a girl and marry her. You obviously can. What I'm saying is that, far too often, men get stuck in a scarcity mindset, because they think that there's only "one girl" for them.

What then happens, is that their neediness and desperation for this one particular girl actually ends up driving her away. This is why I tell any newbies to the game to go sleep with 10 women before you even think of settling down with a girlfriend.

If you picked up this book, maybe you're currently trying to get over a oneitis. Perhaps you're stuck on an ex-girlfriend, or even worse, a girl you haven't even slept with yet, but who you're obsessed over. If this is the case, I advise you to make a Tinder and start approaching at least 5 girls a day, minimum, for the next 30 days.

The "oneitis" comes from putting a girl up on a pedestal. It comes from associating your internalized "goddess figure," which is a Jungian archetype, with a real-life woman. In other words, on some sort of subconscious level, you actually believe she's a goddess among women.

While this may seem romantic, it's actually incredibly repulsive to women. They want a man who has abundance, and who isn't

33

obsessed over her to the point of desperation. You must always be willing to walk away as a man, otherwise, you risk an unhealthy, codependent relationship with a woman.

When she senses that you will never leave her, she will likely begin to resent you, and slowly start to walk all over you. Again, it pains me to say this, but it's true – you've been lied to. The way to a woman's heart is not to treat her as a goddess, but rather to treat her as a human being, like the rest of us. She's not special – even if she's a perfect 10.

She still shits. She still eats. She still probably farts after a night of drinking tequila and munching on some Taco Bell. Never forget this – don't put her on a pedestal and make her the oneitis.

Chapter 3: The 5 Stages of Red Pill

Upon hearing these truths, many men go through what I've deemed the "5 Stages of Red Pill," named after the "5 Stages of Grief." In it, men experience five distinct phases:

1. Denial
2. Anger
3. Bargaining
4. Depression
5. Acceptance

Each phase is marked by a distinct outlook on reality, a specific emotion, and a clear view of women. As I said before in one of my videos, you must go through the "5 Stages of Red Pill" in order to get over any anger you might have towards women.

Stage 1. Denial

Upon first being exposed to these truths, most men vehemently deny them. Thankfully, today's youth aren't as brainwashed as the previous generation, but even so, many still cannot accept these fundamental truths about women and the dating marketplace.

Women are emotional. They prefer to fuck alpha males. They will sometimes use men for their financial resources, and you must guard yourself against this. You should never put a woman as your purpose, because she will begin to resent you.

These are all self-evident truths, that are deeply ingrained in us, on a biological level. They cannot be undone, they cannot be rewritten, and they must not be ignored.

Unfortunately, however, most men have been brainwashed for years to believe the following:

- Women are just as emotional as men
- Men should put a woman as the #1 priority in his life
- Having sex with your girlfriend once a month is normal
- You should always be a "good boy" and listen to your girlfriend

While it's painfully apparent that these statements are ludicrous, most men are fed these beliefs from birth, to the point that denying them would be taken as heresy. This is why most men initially deny the red pill truths discussed above.

They cannot imagine, even for a second, that their "good girl" Susie, who they spent 3 months dating before she put out, would EVER in her right mind, fuck some "Chad" for a one-night stand. And yet, this type of thing happens every day.

As you experience the truths written in this book for yourself, and as you begin to unravel the beta programming you've undergone, you will identify other men in your lives who are in the "denial" phase. Do not try to change their minds. They must go through this journey alone.

Stage 2. Anger

The second phase that men go through, after being exposed to the truth about women, is the anger phase. "How dare you call my girlfriend a slut! What do you mean she's had one night stands before!? She told me she was a virgin!"

As men wake up to the truth, they grow furious. "You're just an incel! A neckbeard living in his Mom's basement! There's no way you've slept with over 150 women! You must have raped them! You're a liar! You're a manipulative pickup artist!"

The list goes on and on...

To assuage their inadequacies, most men will just blame others. Rather than acknowledging the "alpha fucks vs. beta bucks" paradigm, they'll simply look at a man such as Dan Bilzerian, and call him a "douchebag" and an "asshole."

It is vital that you do not succumb to anger. Yes, I understand many of these truths can be hard to swallow. I know it can sometimes be difficult to know there are other guys out there, who fucked your girlfriend within an hour of meeting her, when she made you wait for three dates before you even got close to fucking her.

I understand it is hard to let go of past beliefs, but it must be done. You now have a choice – you can run back to the blue pill, like a coward, and ignore the red pilled truth, or you can move forward, and use the truth to better guide your actions. I chose the latter.

Stage 3. Bargaining

After getting past the anger phase, most men begin to "bargain" with reality. They'll try to accept certain parts of the truth, in exchange for also mixing it with a lie. "Well, I guess some women are hypergamous... but not all of them are!" they'll say. "Maybe YOUR girl will test you, but mine would never do such a thing!"

While this isn't ideal, at least the truth is starting to sink in. This is a normal process for anyone exposed to controversial new realities. It takes time to accept the truth.

"Well, maybe your girl is hypergamous, but mine loves me for who I am! I can just be a fat, lazy piece of shit, and she won't lose interest in me at all!" Give me a break.

Most women do not want to settle – and while there are some "exceptions" or "unicorns" as they're sometimes called, it's often not a matter of black/white, but simply "how much."

Can you find a loyal girl? Yes. Can you find girls who will willingly build a family with you, and forego other, even "better" opportunities? Of course. Is it hard to do, however? You bet.

Stage 4. Depression

After the bargaining stage, most men grow depressed over many things. They get depressed that women aren't really as logical as they thought, that women have been cheating on them behind their backs, and that they've been lied to their entire lives.

This is normal. It's hard not to get depressed when these things happen. But, as always, you must trudge on. This may be the most difficult phase to get past when swallowing the red pill, simply because it is so persistent. Everywhere you look, you will begin to see confirmation that these truths hold true.

You'll look at past girlfriends and see how your relationship fell apart when you stopped being an alpha male. You'll notice how they tested you, and you didn't even realize it. You'll notice that your high school sweetheart ended up fucking Chad, because she's hypergamous.

Eventually, however, you will accept these things.

Stage 5. Acceptance

Once you reach the phase of acceptance, the world is your oyster. While it may be difficult to swallow the red pill, once you do so, everything will start to make sense. No longer will you be operating in the dark – instead you'll be able to formulate a specific game plan for success.

You're not dating enough women? Time to employ some red pill advice on approaching, attracting, and sleeping with women (which we will discuss later in this book). Your girl keeps testing you? It's because she wants to see if you truly are as confident as you seem.

Now, women will no longer be a mystery to you. In fact, they'll often be incredibly predictable. Once you get these basic, fundamental tenets down, you will understand women.

Part 2: What Women Want

"Attraction is not a choice."

-David DeAngelo

"Women want a man who is a leader. They want a man who's decisive, confident, and has firm boundaries. In other words, they want an alpha male."

-Jon Anthony

Executive Summary

Do not trust a woman when she says what she wants. Most people are woefully unaware of what they truly want in life, and will give you one answer while acting out another. While some women are self-aware enough to know what they're attracted to, most are not.

Fundamentally, there are four basic desires, which all women crave. These are resources, status, personality, and looks. What women prefer in the long-term is different than what they prefer in the short-term, however.

In the long-term, status and resources will be screened for more heavily, whereas in the short-term, most women focus primarily on your personality (game) and your looks.

The "Alpha Male" is an archetype used to define what women want. Basically, there are two parts of the alpha male: the inner and the outer.

The "inner characteristics" of the alpha male are true confidence, congruence, non-neediness, clarity of intent, presence, carefree energy, and a bigger purpose. The outer" characteristics" of the alpha male are good grooming, good style, and good hygiene.

If you wish to maximize your success with women, it is paramount that you do not neglect any of these areas. Getting to the top 1% of men requires that you become a holistic, well-rounded man, who has all areas of his life in order.

Chapter 4. Why You Should Never Trust Women for Dating Advice

Ah, here we go... now into the good stuff. So now that we understand a few basic principles of female behavior, it's time to ask the question: what do women want?

Why is this important? It's simple. If you know what women want, you can become this very thing, and then rather than wanting someone else, they will want you.

So please, pay close attention... because this may be one of the most important parts of this entire book. The first thing you need to know is that you should NEVER trust a woman when she tells you what she wants.

Why? Well, it's not because she's lying. Rather, it's because she's emotional, and half the time women don't even know what they want. Think about it – even when you ask men what they want in life, they'll give you some answer like: "I want to be a millionaire."

But then when you look at their behavior, do they act in such a way that will make them a millionaire? Of course not. Most men who say they want to be a millionaire will be perfectly content working a shitty 9-5 job and never starting a business.

It's the same with women. They THINK they know what they want, but most of the time, they really don't. Of course, there are times where a woman is self-aware enough to know what she wants, but more often than not, you'll get a vague, generic answer such as:

- "I want a really nice guy who takes me out on dates!"
- "I want Mr. Tall, Dark, and Handsome!"

- "I want to date a guy who buys me flowers. Lots of flowers."

Yet, when you look at the guys these girls are actually dating, more often than not they don't do any of these things. Now don't get me wrong – I'm not saying you shouldn't be a good guy and take your girlfriend out on dates, or that you shouldn't buy her flowers. It just has to come from the right place, which we'll talk about as this book goes on.

When a girl says she wants something, she genuinely does want it... in that moment. But that doesn't mean she's ATTRACTED to it. In other words, if she's dating "Mr. Bad Boy," and she's obsessed with him, what do you think she'll say she wants? Probably a nice guy.

Does this mean she actually wants a nice guy? Of course not. It simply means she's frustrated that "Mr. Bad Boy" won't act like "Mr. Nice Guy." What she doesn't realize though, is that this is the very reason she's attracted to him. He's wild, he's untamable, and he's an alpha.

As you go through your dating journey, you will likely have many girls try to "tame" you. And while this may be appropriate when you're ready to settle down, you are under no circumstances to give your own life up to please her. You are the master of your own kingdom, and you must have a queen who is willing to submit to your rule – not the other way around.

Chapter 5. Short Term vs. Long Term Attraction Triggers

Now that we've got that out of the way, let's get into what women actually want from a guy. Do they want stability or excitement? An asshole or a nice guy? Wealth and riches, or stunning good looks? Unfortunately, it's not that simple.

As I said before, women are evolutionarily programmed to crave the best genetics, while at the same time, securing a man who is willing to provide for them. This leads to the "lover/provider" dynamic, and it also leads to different desires for different time frames.

In other words, what women often want in the *short run* is a lot different than what women want in the *long term.* You might get mad, but are men any different? Would you like to date and marry a sexy, naughty stripper, who can fuck you all night long, but is a wild, dramatic, chaotic mess? Of course not. Would you like to bang her for a few months, though? Undoubtedly.

Women are no different. Often, what they're looking for will change with their age. This is important to keep in mind as you date different women. Personally, I usually date girls who are 5-6 years younger than me (in the 18-21 age bracket), because they often aren't looking for anything serious. To be fair, some are, but most are focused on college.

So, with this in mind, let's get into what women want...

The 4 Desires

There're four basic things that women want in me
before, the EMPHASIS on these things will change depending on
her age and time frame, but overall, here they are:

1. Resources (Money, Connections, etc.)
2. Status (Male Dominance Hierarchy)
3. Personality (Game, Competence, etc.)
4. Looks (Handsome, Height, etc.)

Each of these is relatively simple to understand, but I will give a quick overview. Your resources are simply things like money, connections, and power. Women are attracted to these things, because given a long enough time frame, they signify a competent, ambitious alpha male, who will be able to protect her.

Status is another powerful attraction trigger. This just means being a "leader of men," as Mystery (AKA Eric Von Markovich) put it. When you show her that other men look up to you, follow your lead, and respect you, it shows her that you're a high-status man.

In tribal times, this meant you could protect her more easily. If she's fucking you and has a child with you, none of the other men will try to harm her or her child, because they all look up to you. If you're the type of man who was at the bottom of the totem pole, however? It would be a much different, much uglier story.

Next, and _most importantly,_ is your personality. This is by far the #1 sticking point that all of my clients have, and that you likely have as well. Some people in the "black pill" community believe that personality is mostly unimportant, but all of my experience proves that it is the #1 priority for women.

Why? It's simple. Your personality CONVEYS your potential to accrue everything else. When you demonstrate extreme confidence, women pick up on this. They ask themselves: "Why is he so confident? Is he rich? Does he have a huge dick? What is it?" They begin to wonder and think about you – and even if you don't have these things, the fact that you have confidence shows you're willing to pursue what you want in life, and you will likely succeed.

I will discuss personality later on, but for now, understand it is the most important aspect out of all these attraction triggers.

Lastly, are your looks. This includes everything from your grooming, your hygiene, and your style, to your height and weight. These are important, because they help you make a great first impression on a girl. If you're good looking, she will be more likely to hear you out for a few minutes, before deciding if she's interested in you or not.

Short Term Attraction Triggers

In the short term, your personality and looks are the most critical factors. Social status and resources play almost no role in attracting a mate short term. They can certainly help, but the primary attraction triggers for women who are living "in the moment" are your looks and your personality (a la your game).

This is why I advise my clients to get their image and their game down, if they're trying to sleep with tons of girls. It's not that having money doesn't help, and it isn't that having high social status doesn't help either. It's merely that focusing your time on maximizing your looks and your personality is the highest leverage point.

If you aren't already, you should be lifting weights regularly. I recommend my own workout routine, called "Body of an Alpha," which will teach you:

- The fast track method to get the "V-Taper" look that will literally make women wet when they see you

46

- My "hybrid training protocol" that sheds fat as it builds slabs of muscle
- My full nutrition layout, including customizable options for your specific body type and needs
- How to get your V-Taper body in 3 months or less, guaranteed

The big problem with most workout programs is they don't give you the kind of body women really want. In gyms today, most guys have the bulky kind of body that literally TURNS WOMEN OFF!

Body of an Alpha was created to give you that lean, shredded physique that women are programmed to want to have sex with. And it will give it to you in the quickest, easiest way possible. Want better results with women? Then I strongly encourage you to check it out.

The goal is to have a lean, shredded physique, with powerful, broad shoulders. This communicates alpha male status to women, and it will draw them to you like magic.

In addition to this, you obviously want to have good style, good hygiene, and good grooming. These things will be discussed throughout this book, but a full guide would be much too cumbersome. That being said, there is also plenty of free advice on my blog.

In addition to your appearance, demonstrating "alpha male characteristics" is another essential thing you must be doing to pull girls in the short term. Things like confidence, dominance, and assertiveness are all powerful aspects to add to your personality.

Long Term Attraction Triggers

In the long run, women pay more attention to your social status and your wealth. Again, if you're trying to date beautiful women for longer periods of time, you should still improve your appearance and your personality. That being said, women place more emphasis on a man's stability and overall status as a provider in the long run.

This is why you will be able to rack up a huge notch count if you're good looking and have good game but may find it difficult to keep a girlfriend. This was my problem for the longest time, but hey, I'm not complaining.

As you date more and more beautiful women, you will start to realize that they want the "full package." They not only want a man who has the "short term attraction triggers" down, but also the long-term ones. Your goal should be to maximize everything you possibly can, so as to provide yourself with the best chances at finding your dream girl.

Chapter 6: Becoming The Alpha Male

If I had to summarize what women want in a single phrase, it would be: "The Alpha Male." This does not do a justice however, as this term has been so convoluted and stereotyped over the years, that it hardly means anything without further explanation.

But just what is an alpha male, and how do we become one? Women are complicated creatures, and thus their wants and needs are more complicated than ours.

The alpha male is one who demonstrates himself superior in all regards – think of him as a sort of "God amongst men." He's more confident than other men. He's more socially calibrated than other men. He's physically superior to other men. He's better than them in every way.

Now, does this mean you have to set yourself up for failure by aiming at some impossible standards? Of course not. No mortal man will ever fully embody the "alpha male" gestalt, but it is more than possible to get close to it.

For the sake of clarity, I've created two sets of characteristics that every alpha male has: inner and outer. The inner alpha male characteristics can be roughly equated to your personality or your game. The outer alpha male characteristics tie into your looks, but they're permeable, so if you were born ugly, don't fret.

The inner alpha characteristics include:

1. True Confidence
2. Congruence
3. Non-Neediness
4. Clarity of Intent
5. Presence
6. Carefree Energy
7. The Bigger Purpose

The outer alpha characteristics include:

1. Grooming
2. Style
3. Hygiene
4. Body Language

Mastering both of these sets of characteristics will be challenging to say the least, but hey, nobody said that becoming a 1% man was easy.

Chapter 7: Alpha Male Personality Traits

If you get anything from this book, make it this: adopting these inner alpha characteristics as your own, will without a doubt, enable you to create the dating life you've always dreamt of. Take notes on these, brainwash yourself to believe these, and tattoo these principles onto your fucking forehead. They will make all the difference.

Why? Again, it's simple. The very first thing a woman notices about you is your looks, but the second thing she notices is your personality. In fact, some women actually notice your personality before they see your looks.

How is this possible? When a woman looks at a man, she's unconsciously scanning him for social information. So, when she sees a man walk with incredible confidence, this will be the first thing that comes to her mind. It's only a few moments later that she'll notice how tall he is, how he looks, what he's wearing, and so on.

In other words, personality will trump looks every single time. It doesn't matter if you're short or ugly – if you walk, talk, and act like you fuck girls as hot as her, she will notice. Trust me on this. Good game will trump good looks 100% of the time.

In fact, that's why I made my very first and best-selling eBook, "7 Strategies to Develop Your Masculinity." I saw that many men kept trying to change their outer appearance and surface-level techniques, without fundamentally changing who they are as a person.

This is what my "7 Strategies" program will teach you, when you buy it now:

- How to skyrocket within yourself what turns women on THE MOST – unbridled masculinity

- How to put out an "Alpha Funk" where hot girls approach YOU
- How to become the most "alpha male" version of yourself, without changing who you are, and without becoming a try-hard douchebag

It's one of the few programs on the market that directly deals with the root cause of most guys' problems with women. When you get your masculinity handled, your success with women will explode.

It's happened for thousands of guys around the globe, and it's about to happen for you, too. It's my unbreakable guarantee, if you do decide to purchase these 7 Strategies.

If you don't, then that's fine, too. There's more than enough information in this book, and on my blog for free, that you can start employing today.

So, with all of that in mind, let's get into just precisely what women are attracted to... the "inner alpha male" characteristics, that when mastered, will explode your dating life.

Trait #1 - True Confidence

Why do I say "true confidence" and not just mere "confidence"? Well, because confidence is a term that's so overused nowadays, it's completely lacking in meaning. The truth is it's pretty hard to define confidence, but if I had to put a definition to it, it would simply be that you are 100%, completely okay with who you are.

I know this sounds cheesy, but this level of confidence is like chick crack. When girls sense that you're completely okay with who you are, and that you aren't putting on any sort of front whatsoever, this is the type of thing that will make them fall madly in love with you.

But, here's the thing – true confidence, and congruence (which we will get to next) is polarizing. In other words, they will force girls to decide if they like you or not. When you're genuinely yourself, girls will be able to tell if they want you or not, within the first few minutes of conversation – and sometimes even faster.

Now, before I go on any further, let me address an often pointed out contradiction:

> *"Hold on, Jon. So, you're saying I'm supposed to be who I truly am? That's what confidence is? Well, I've been doing that for the last 10 years of my life and haven't gotten any girls due to it. How is this supposed to help me?"*

Oh, you poor fool... let me explain. Most men think they're being true to themselves, but the matter of fact is that they actually aren't. They've constructed a series of fake identities, to avoid social judgment from their friends, their coworkers, and their bosses. In other words, most people have been living a lie for so long, they've forgotten it's a lie in the first place.

That band you think you really like? You started listening to them in 8th grade, because all the cool kids were talking about them. You never actually liked them, you just said you did for so long, that you actually internalized that lie as a truth.

You sitting at home, watching Netflix, and refusing to go out and meet new chicks? That's not because you really like binge-watching The Office for the five millionth time. It's because you're afraid to go out. Are you starting to see the point here?

Most guys live in a state of constant fear. They're afraid of getting rejected, so they never approach a girl they think is beautiful. They're afraid of going broke, so they never start the business they've always wanted to start. They're so scared of damn near everything, that they bottle themselves up and hide away from the world, developing a thick outer shell.

True confidence is vulnerable. Mark Manson has a great book on this concept called Models. The whole idea is that the way you actually attract women is by being vulnerable. I know it may be hard to accept this, so let me tell you a story to really help this concept sink in.

I was lying in bed with a beautiful, black-haired woman, after a crazy-passionate sex session. She stared deep into my eyes, and asked me a question: "Are you a good person?"

Rather than just rattling off some stupid answer that most guys would give, I actually thought about it. I thought about it for what felt like hours, then I finally responded: "I try to be."

She gazed into my soul, and spoke thus: "Then that means you are."

I could see her eyes grow wide, as her pupils dilated (a sign that a girl is falling in love with you). My honesty – my complete, unfettered honesty – had turned her on.

Some of you may be rolling your eyes right now, but that's the type of conversation that drives women wild. They want to see who you are – they want you to bare your soul to them. And the way you do this, is by being 100% confident with who you are as a man.

Confidence also manifests itself as fearlessness. When you're confident in who you are, why would you ever be afraid of anything? A man who is confident in himself, trusts himself to always make the right decisions, and thus he's never scared.

He sees a beautiful woman? He has no problem walking right up to her and asking her out on the spot. He has something on his mind, and wants to say it? Then he says it. True confidence can be

54

spotted a mile away, and in fact, it is the core of what women find attractive.

...but why do they find this confidence so intoxicating? I've thought long and hard about this, and the simplest and most honest answer, is because it connects with her on a deep and primal level. When you think of a God amongst men – a Zeus, a Hercules, or a King Leonidas – do you picture a weak bitch who's afraid of who they are?

Of course not. You envision a man who lives as fearlessly as he dies; a man who lives fully, and acts, talks, and breathes with a consistent message: I am here, and this is who I am.

For those of you who prefer a more scientific answer, the reason is that true confidence is always a signifier of high status. Again, let's rewind the clock some 20,000 years. We're all in tribes, and we're fighting for our survival. Each day brings new uncertainties, and none of us truly know if we'll live to see the next day or not.

In this type of a situation, do you think a man at the bottom of the totem pole can afford to truly speak his mind? Of course not. Say one thing that pisses off the leader of the tribe, and you're hosed – your genes will be wiped out of existence faster than you can say "Hoohah."

The leader of the pack, however? He can say whatever he damn well pleases. He has no fear of rejection, because no one dares to reject him. This is why true confidence is, and will always be, a signifier of high status.

Trait #2 - Congruence

Similar to true confidence, is congruence. This just means being aligned in your thoughts, words, and actions. Again, why is this attractive? Because it communicates fearlessness, which is always an indicator of high status.

When you're congruent, you aren't afraid to be who you truly are. In many ways, this is identical to confidence – yet I decided to make it a separate trait, to emphasize a key point.

Confidence is what ENABLES congruence, but they are not the same thing. Without confidence, you cannot be congruent – that's why it's so important to develop confidence in your life, through continually proving yourself and overcoming challenges.

Do not buy into the bullshit "self-help" idea that confidence can be built by meditating and sitting around all day – it can't. Instead, if you want to truly build confidence in who you are as a man, you must face challenges that you are afraid of, and overcome them.

Anyways, back to congruence. Congruence is when you are aligned in your thoughts, words, and actions. It's when you speak, feel, and LIVE by your truth. Take for example, the Amish. Despite what you may think of their religion, you cannot deny that they are congruent. Every day, they live the way that their religion dictates.

When the sun comes up, they go out to the fields. When the sun goes down, they go inside with their families. Every Sunday, they spend time with their community at church. This is the way of life for them, and it's congruent with who they are.

Likewise, in order for you to be congruent, everything in your life must be aligned. Does your job fit your personality? Does your home match up with who you are? If not, this is fine... but it is always something you must be striving for.

The best place to start, is congruence with your true feelings and thoughts. It's being honest with yourself, and with others. I know this might sound like some woo-woo self-help bullshit, but the truth is it's not. People CRAVE authenticity. In a world of fakers and liars, finally meeting someone who is unapologetically who they are, is incredibly refreshing.

Trait #3 - Non-Neediness

If you're a regular reader of my blog, you've likely heard me talk a lot about non-neediness before. Non-neediness simply means that you do not need her to feel validated. It means that you are perfectly fine with who you are as a man, and you do not require her validation to feel good about yourself.

In other words, maybe you tell a girl you're into Led Zeppelin, and maybe she says that she hates them. It should not affect you one way or another, because you do not need her to agree with you to feel good about yourself. You just are who you are.

Far too often, guys will demonstrate needy behavior by CONSTANTLY chasing after a girl who does not reciprocate their interest. We've all done it before, too. Maybe you meet a girl who's absolutely stunning, and for whatever reason, she isn't into you. Yet, you keep texting her, calling her, and trying to get a hold of her, when she offers almost nothing in return.

This type of behavior repels women, because it communicates that you feel as if you need her. You are not centered in your masculine energy, and you feel that without her validation, you are less as a man. Instead, the best way to win a woman's heart over, is to be persistent, but non-needy.

Do not get upset if she doesn't text you back. Don't get angry at her if she takes a few days to get back to you. The best approach in the beginning stages of dating is relative emotional detachment. Now, this doesn't mean you can't go deep with a woman, if you both genuinely connect with each other on an intimate level. But women take time to fall in love. You would be wise to keep this in mind, as you go about your dating life.

Non-neediness can be cultivated through meditation, being on your purpose, and having your own life aside from her. If you want to be happy – truly happy – as a man, you must have your own passions, hobbies, and life apart from hers. This includes friends, family gatherings, and maybe even other girls you're dating.

Women are attracted to abundance, in all of its forms – material abundance, emotional abundance, and energetic abundance. When you communicate that you are a man who is non-needy, you communicate to her that you have abundance.

Trait #4 - Clarity of Intent

Another important aspect of being an alpha male is having clarity of intent. Go out to night clubs sometime, and you'll see this in action. You'll see tons of guys approach girls, with the obvious intention of sleeping with them, but they're so afraid of being sexual. They're afraid of being too direct. They're afraid of being a man.

This doesn't mean to walk up to a girl, and instantly try to stick your dick inside her – but she should know, and more importantly, FEEL, why you're approaching her. Your intention, which is presumably to sleep with her, must be clearly communicated by your body language. If you are attracted to her, do not be afraid to hide it. Women go crazy for this.

They know why you're approaching them – they aren't stupid. Beautiful women know that when you walk up to them, as a complete stranger, it's probably because you want to sleep with them. Now, this doesn't mean you shouldn't screen them –

screen hard. Don't simply be willing to fuck them under any and all circumstances. They must pass your criteria.

I typically approach girls with the frame of: "Hey, you're sexy, and I wanted to meet you and see what you're like in person." That's it. Do you see how that frame is far more powerful than something like: "Hey, I want to fuck, will you please fuck me?"

This way, you aren't the seller, but rather more of the buyer. You don't need to have sex with her if she demonstrates rudeness, bitchiness, or any other characteristics you dislike. You can choose to walk away at any moment.

Clarity of intent, again, just means that you are aligned in your thoughts, words, and actions. You know exactly what you want, and you are taking action to get it. This is where the old saying: "Ask and you shall receive" comes from.

What's funny too, is that as you begin to experiment with this concept, you will realize how easy it is to get what you want in life. Things will just magically happen, as if some "higher force" or "universal law" is bringing them about for you.

Have you ever noticed that when you tell someone to do something, and you REALLY mean it, they typically do it? For example, if you see a pedestrian about to get hit by a car, and so you yell: "STOP!" they will typically stop, no? Why is this? It's because they sensed the authenticity in your voice – the urgency, the confidence, and the dominance.

If you yelled out meekly: "Stop? Please?" they would probably completely ignore you, because you aren't clear in your intent. Part of you wants them to stop, part of you is worried they won't stop, and another part of you is worried that maybe they shouldn't stop.

When you're clear in your intent, women respond favorably. Most guys have one foot on the "gas," and one foot on the "brakes," because they're terrified of approaching her. While some level of approach anxiety is normal, with practice, you can actually turn it into excitement.

Trait #5 - Presence

A true alpha male is present and exists in the now. When you picture a beta male 50,000 years ago, living in our theoretical tribe, you probably imagine someone who's always worrying about shit. "Oh jeez, I wonder if Susie likes me! I hope Grok doesn't get mad at me again! Oh man, will it ever rain again? I haven't been able to catch a deer in so long..."

The beta male is not present. He is thinking about things left and right, and because of it, his ability to act in the present moment is weakened. A good book on this is The Power of Now by Eckhart Tolle. It discusses how the most powerful thing you can do, is to actually stop worrying, and just focus on the present moment.

This doesn't mean you can't use thoughts – don't be a fool. But rather than using thoughts to serve them, most people are used by their thoughts. They spend all day worrying about this and about that, without ever really doing anything about them.

Do you think Chad Thundercock, the alpha male caveman, is worrying about what Susie thinks or about what will happen tomorrow? Of course not. He's present. He's happy. He doesn't have any concerns for the future, and even if he does, he only thinks about them momentarily to think of a plan on how to deal with them, and then he executes on the plan.

When you aren't present, it means you are a slave to your thoughts. You are a slave to your emotions. Do not be like this. I recommend men meditate for at least five minutes a day. You may want to start off small just to build the habit, but eventually grow it into 10 or 20 minutes a day, to get the most benefit for the least amount of time investment.

When you are present with a girl, she can feel it in her very being. She can notice it in your eyes. She wants you to be with her – here and now. Not off in some fairyland. She wants to see the way your eyes look deep into hers, and she wants to feel your presence as a man.

Trait #6 - Carefree

Another critical characteristic of all alpha males is their "devil may care" attitude. They aren't affected by the same laws that most people follow. In other words, they're fearless. They aren't afraid that this might happen, or that might happen. Instead, they're carefree.

This doesn't mean to do stupid things and throw all caution to the wind. Rather, it means acknowledging that you will die one day, and our time here is very short, so you might as well live life to the fullest and treat it as if it's an adventure.

When you adopt a carefree attitude, women are drawn to you like bees to honey. Everyone is living stressful lives these days, afraid of paying their bills, fearful of what will happen tomorrow, and afraid of living life. The man who is free to dictate his own emotions, and rather than choosing fear, chooses to be happy, adventurous, and carefree, will have his pick of women.

Think of the alpha males and the beta males, sitting around the fire. Chad Grok is the best hunter in all of the tribe, and he's known for his prowess in battle. All the girls want him, and he routinely feasts upon the buffalo and wild animals he killed earlier, and the pussy as well.

Do you think Chad Grok is worried if he couldn't find an animal to kill today? Of course not. Why would he be? He has the best hunting skills in all of the land. He's a king! He doesn't need to worry, because come tomorrow, when he finds another animal, he will kill it and feast.

Jerry the Beta Caveman, however? He's always worried. He's never carefree and adventurous, because he can't afford to be. One little slip up and he could go hungry for the next month, or get his arm ripped off by a Sabre-Toothed Tiger.

The case is clear – alpha males are carefree. They don't worry, because ultimately, it doesn't even matter! Now, I know what you may be thinking:

> *"But Jon, aren't there things you should worry about? Isn't it important that we admit certain things in life are bad, and that we don't want them to happen?"*

Of course! There are many bad things that we don't want to happen, but does worrying about them ever cause this to change? No, of course not. All that worry does is drain your mental energy and turn your focus onto something that isn't productive.

Every great truth is, in some sense, a paradox. On the one hand, there are definitely things we don't want to happen. We don't want to lose our jobs, we don't want to lose our girlfriends, and we don't want the world to erupt in World War III. But on the other hand, worrying does absolutely nothing to solve these problems, or to make them less likely.

The only sensible way to deal with problems is to admit they are real, form an action plan to deal with them, and execute on the action plan. That's it. This is what the Chad alpha males of the world understand, and it's what the Jerry Beta Groks do not.

Trait #7 - Bigger Purpose

The two most important points out of this entire list, in my opinion, are having confidence and having a bigger purpose. If you can just master these two things alone, then most of the others will follow, and women will be irresistibly drawn towards you.

Confidence is important, because without it, you will not feel capable of achieving your purpose. Your purpose is essential however, because without it, you will have no direction, and consequently, no reason to live.

Without a purpose, men are like a sailboat in the middle of the ocean. There is no left, there is no right, and there is no up or down. There is just chaos. A vast, endless, tumultuous sea of uncertainty. Most men nowadays have lost their purpose... and I'm here to change this.

When you discover your purpose, everything becomes clear. You wake up, and rather than feeling tired, groggy, and depressed, you feel energized. When you go through your day, you are fueled by 100% focus and vision. And when you go to sleep at night? Well, you don't even WANT to go to sleep, because your purpose has set your soul on fire.

There have been times in my life, where I literally feel as if I'm ancient – I'm timeless. I'm the spirit of God, the Universe, Father Time, and Mother Nature incarnate. These experiences are incredible, and when you follow your purpose, you will have them regularly. You start to realize that the whole world is your oyster, and you can accomplish anything you want.

As a man, you must have a bigger purpose. Even if your bigger purpose is only to "make $5,000 a month so I can move out of my parents' house," you need SOMETHING that will set a fire under your ass in the mornings and get you out of bed. You need something to give you the motivation to dig deep, when the going gets tough.

It doesn't matter if you aren't 100% convinced something is your purpose. I get questions like this all the time, from readers all across the world:

> *"Jon, I've tried to find my purpose, but I just can't seem to find it. Nothing motivates me like you say it should and lights a fire under my ass like you mention. How do I find it?"*

My answer is always the same: you don't need to get it perfect the first time around. Just create a goal that you can get behind, create a PLAN to achieve that goal, and start taking action. Again, even if it's something as small as "I want to lose 15 pounds of fat and gain 5 pounds of muscle" or "I want to find a girlfriend this year," will do.

It doesn't matter if your purpose is some gigantic thing or not. Your purpose will continually change as you grow, adapt, and evolve in the world. The important thing is that you start orienting yourself towards a goal and purpose though, because as you achieve these goals, you will begin to set your sights higher and higher, and eventually, find your ultimate purpose.

Women find this type of ambitious attitude in a man absolutely intoxicating. Why? Because there is no greater predictor of success than AMBITION. If a woman can find a man who is ambitious, if she is willing to support him, they can accomplish just about anything together.

Women love playing a supportive role in a man's life, and when you show her that you're a champion worth supporting, she will become addicted to helping you grow. They've done studies on this actually, where they'll present women with two types of men:

1. A wealthy young man who inherited his money, but who isn't particularly intelligent, hard-working, ambitious, or competent
2. A broke young man who has no money, but who is extremely ambitious, motivated, hard-working, and goal-oriented

In almost every single example, the women chose the second man. Why is this? Most men believe that women are attracted to a wealthy man... and as I said in previous chapters, in some sense, they are. But do you know what they're attracted to more than wealth?

The PROMISE of wealth. Nothing is more fulfilling for a woman, than to find a young, ambitious, motivated man, to pair up with him, and to help him accomplish his goals. Nothing is more spiritually, emotionally, and sexually satisfying for a woman than this.

Think of the men that women want to fuck. James Bond, Christian Grey, the captain of the football team... they all have a firm sense of purpose and are goal-driven. Fundamentally, masculine energy is directive. It is like a freight training speeding down the tracks at 150 miles per hour, and it will not let anything in its tracks stop it from getting where it wants to be.

Masculinity is like a raging bull, charging through the fields – a thousand pounds of raw, brute strength, stampeding inexorably to whatever its eyes are set on. And when you create this bigger purpose, and sense of direction for yourself? Girls will be drawn to you like wildfire.

Chapter 8. Alpha Male Appearance

In addition to embodying the inner alpha male characteristics, it also helps to have good outer alpha male characteristics. These are things like grooming, style, and hygiene.

In general, girls don't look so much at your "looks" but rather your "image." Your image is more so what you DO with your looks. In other words, it doesn't matter that much if you're traditionally attractive or not. What matters is that you know how to work with what you've got.

Good Grooming (Hairstyles)

One of the first things a woman will notice, is if you have good grooming or not. This includes your facial hair, your hairstyle, and other miscellaneous things such as if your nails are kempt, if your body hair is clean, and if your eyebrows are well shaped.

Why is this so attractive? Well, let's go back a few million years to take a look at our chimpanzee ancestors. Studies have shown that the alpha male chimps consistently have large numbers of female chimps grooming their hair. They'll pick the lice out of their hair, detangle it, and pull the dirt and loose bits out as well.

So how does this translate to humans? In short, when you have good grooming, it's a powerful sub-communicator of pre-selection (that you have other girls). It goes deep into a woman's caveman DNA, that when she sees a man who's very well groomed, she unconsciously becomes more attracted to him.

You don't have to spend a fortune to look good, but spending a little bit of money certainly helps. For example, take a look at the following image. Notice how even though this man isn't particularly handsome, his hairstyle accentuates his good facial features, and is very crisp, clean, and well maintained.

Do you see how all of the edges are well-groomed? His hair is split nicely, it's brushed over to the side, and it just seems to "fit" with his look. This is what I mean when I say good grooming.

Take a look at this other image below. Notice how his hairstyle fades nicely on the side, and then how his facial hair accentuates this fade. This is an example of how you can combine your hairstyle and your facial hair to create a "look," or your "image."

Notice how his grooming is on point, however. His hair is clean, there are no random bits of hair sticking out of place, and it all just seems to "flow" naturally. This is the type of look that women want – not necessarily a certain "type" of hair (long, short, curly, straight) but rather that you maximize your own PERSONAL looks, into your "image."

Here are a few more examples of some good hairstyles.

Do you see how all of these hairstyles create a certain "look"? It's important that your hairstyle be congruent with who you are as a person. Otherwise, it will look out of place. For example, if you're a hardcore punk rocker type guy, you probably want a more edgy haircut. Likewise, if you're a more reserved guy, you probably want a more conservative haircut.

In addition to matching your hairstyle with your image, you also want to keep in mind that certain hairstyles will either make your face look good or bad. Take a look at the picture down below, which classifies your face shape into six different categories.

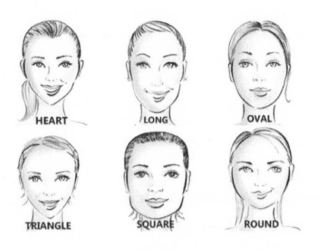

Depending on your face shape, you will look better in different hairstyles. If you have, for example, a round face, putting some height into your hairstyle will balance it out. In contrast, if you have a longer face, putting some width into your hairstyle might not be a bad idea.

Any stylist who is worth her salt will typically know these things. That's why I recommend most men get an expensive haircut (at least, at first) to get a good idea of what a proper hairstyle for you SHOULD look like. To find a great stylist, simply follow the prices.

Generally speaking, good stylists will charge you upwards of $50-60 for a men's haircut, with the top stylists charging upwards of $100. Don't worry though, you don't need to pay $100 every time you want to get a haircut. Instead, just get a nice haircut from a good stylist once, and take a picture. Show it to your regular barber the next time you see him, and tell him you want your hair to look just like that.

For a men's shampoo, I recommend you use Biotin Shampoo. It's BPA-free, cruelty-free, smells great, cleans your hair phenomenally, and has an incredible lineup of anti-hair loss ingredients. It blocks DHT, which is the primary hormone which leads to hair loss, meaning that it will literally stop you from balding over the years.

It's also got biotin in it, which is an important chemical that hair needs to grow into its full, lush, and long potential. I use it daily, and cannot recommend it enough.

Good Grooming (Facial Hair)

In addition to having a good hairstyle, having great facial hair is going to also help you with the ladies. It doesn't matter if you can't grow a beard – that's fine. If you can't, then simply stay clean-shaven, or have a small bit of "scruff" if you can pull this look off.

Studies show that women MOST favor a man who has some five o'clock shadow, so if you can attain this look (seen in the picture below), then go for it.

If not, again, that's fine. You can just go clean-shaven. As a miscellaneous pro-tip (which I love to give), if you want to grow a beard but can't, there's still hope. Users on the internet have found that if you rub "minoxidil," which is a hair-regrowth chemical used in "Rogaine," on your face, you can actually start growing a beard within 3-6 months.

To start growing a beard (when you can't grow one), simply rub a small amount of this stuff on the parts of your face where you want to grow the beard, each morning and evening, until you start to see more hair growth. According to users, you'll notice improvements within a month.

For me, I like to keep a little bit of scruff on my face. So rather than shaving it each week, and waiting for it to grow back, I just use a beard trimmer. That way I can keep it at a nice length and never have to worry about it getting "too long" or having to shave it all off (which I hate doing).

Personally, I recommend the Philips Norelco Multigroom. Some of their models are defective and don't work very well, but the one I linked to is great, and it's lasted me over a year so far. I cannot recommend it enough if you hate shaving and want to keep your five o'clock stubble.

The biggest thing about growing a beard, and using your manly facial hair to be more attractive, is that it needs to be well kempt. Take, for example, the classic example of a neckbeard loser. Why is this example so funny? Because his neckbeard is EXTREMELY unkempt. It's gross, unwashed, unclean, and not kept in line.

Do you see why it's so unattractive? He's literally signaling to potential mates that he's a low-value male. He's signaling that he has no "female chimps" to groom his beard, and is, in short, a low-status male. This is obviously not good for your dating life, and must be resolved at once.

Take a look at some of the following examples of GOOD grooming, on the other hand. Notice how all of these beards are well-kempt. They're clean, they're groomed well, there's no random bits and pieces, there aren't any chunks or missing gaps, and they just look "nice" overall.

Again, do you notice how they're all well-kempt? This is the look you want to go for. It doesn't matter if you have a goatee, some five o'clock stubble, or a full-blown beard, what matters is that it's well-kempt, clean, not patchy, and that it matches your look.

Good Grooming (Body Hair)

I don't want to dwell too much on grooming, because I think most of it is pretty obvious. Keep your nails clean, and keep them short. Just follow common sense, and generally speaking, you'll be spot on. That being said, there are a few more things I need to cover.

When it comes to body hair, it's the type of thing you typically won't notice until it's too late. Say, for example, you never shave your genitals. Well, that might work just fine for you, but when you bring that sexy girl home, and she sees your giant unkempt bush, you are going to wish you put some time and effort into keeping it cut.

To keep it short and sweet, I recommend keeping the following areas trimmed:

- Armpits
- Chest
- Pubic Hair
- Ass Hair

To trim these parts of my body, I use a Wahl Model 79602. I do NOT recommend you try any other one, even if it is cheaper. Trust me – I've gone through literally 3-4 different body hair trimmers, and they all sucked shit. They barely even worked, and I threw them out almost immediately. I don't even have a lot of body hair either. They were just cheap and low quality.

Use that electric razor on the parts previously mentioned, and in addition to that, I recommend keeping the following areas CLEAN SHAVEN:

- Ball Sack
- Ass Crack

Yeah, I know it's crude – but trust me, nobody wants hair in their ass. It's annoying. When you take a dump, it gets nasty. Just shave it. I personally use a safety razor to shave my face, my ball sack, and my ass crack.

I don't recommend you start on your ball sack, though. Use it to shave your face first (don't worry, you can replace the razors in between shaves). Get used to using it on your face, get used to the way it cuts, and the angle to use it at, and then consider using it on your other parts. Believe me, you do not want to get cut down there.

Good Style

Next up, is good style. Good style is a little bit like good grooming – there's really no hard and fast rules, but there are general "principles" that you want to follow. The first of which is that you always want your style to match your personality.

Take me, for example. I'm a pretty outspoken man (in case you can't tell). So, do you think I wear nice, fruity colors? Of course not. I wear leather jackets, badass necklaces, and cool, sleek watches. It matches who I am as a person.

I'm also a bit of a gym bro. So, much of my style consists of wearing tank tops, and some sleek gym pants, which compliment my figure. I've found that girls don't care so much what you're wearing, but rather that it's all congruent to your "look."

In my opinion, good style comes down to three main things, and you should master all of them:

1. Clothing
2. Shoes
3. Accessories

If you can learn to match these three things appropriately, you will be just fine. For men, it is helpful to think of clothing as having four main categories:

1. Upper Base Layer (T-Shirts, Dress Shirts, etc.)
2. Lower Base Layer (Shorts, Pants, Jeans, etc.)
3. Outerwear (Jackets, Peacoats, etc.)
4. Miscellaneous (Gloves, Underwear, Socks, etc.)

You typically want to have one of each, unless it's very nice outside, in which case you can skip the outerwear piece. Even so, your outfit will look more "complete" if you have some outerwear.

If you get anything out of this chapter, make it this. Your style should come down to the following three characteristics, and you should master all of them:

1. Good Fit
2. Matching Colors
3. Congruence

If you're lacking in ANY of these things, your style will look out of place. The first and most important thing you need to do, is make sure your clothes FIT. Without a good fit, your clothes will just look stupid on you. This is why most guys are lacking in the fashion department. Statistically speaking, most guys buy two sizes too large.

Personally, I get a lot of my clothes from BYLT Basics. Everything they sell is made explicitly for guys who work out and have an athletic build. This means that, if you lift like I recommend you do, you will look PHENOMENAL in their clothing.

My favorite things I've bought from them are their drop cut T-shirts and their premium joggers. They're both incredibly comfortable, form-fitting, and stylish. In fact, I have multiple shirts and joggers from them, in 3-4 different colors, so they're easy to match with everything else.

Of course, you can always go into stores in person and try their sizes on. Unfortunately, this is really the only way to know if something will fit you for sure. That being said, if I see something I like, I'm not afraid to order it online, and then just return it later for a different size if need be.

Okay – now that this is out of the way, let's talk about matching colors. The biggest cardinal sin that guys commit is matching BROWN accessories with BLACK accessories. This is a big no-no.

So, in other words, if you have a brown belt, you want to have a brown, leather-strapped watch, and a brown pair of shoes.

If you have a black leather jacket, you want to have black boots, and a black belt. Generally speaking, the rule is that you match your shoes with your belt, and if applicable, you can also match your jacket with those two items as well.

I recommend that every guy have a sort of "base wardrobe," which is a collection of some basic, but necessary articles of clothing, that can easily be matched to make great outfits.

A great example of this is like having your kitchen stocked with the right ingredients. You don't need much to make a great dish, just a few types of meat, some spices, and maybe some vegetables along with rice or pasta. Just with those few ingredients, you can make a handful of masterpiece dishes.

Likewise, simply having a few critical articles of clothing can go a long way. I recommend you purchase the items below, because they're a solid "foundation" for your wardrobe:

- Shirts
  - Black T-Shirt (Recommended: Bylt Basics Drop Cut T-Shirt)
  - White T-Shirt (Recommended: Bylt Basics Drop Cut T-Shirt)
  - Black Long Sleeve Shirt (Recommended: Bylt Basics Drop Cut Shirt)
  - White Long Sleeve Shirt (Recommended: Bylt Basics Drop Cut Shirt)
- Pants
  - Basic Dark Denim Jeans (Recommended: Levi Strauss Signature)
  - Basic Black Joggers (Recommended: Bylt Basics Premium Joggers)
- Socks

- o Basic Ankle Socks (Recommended: Champion Double Dry No-Show Socks)
- Jackets
  - o Black Leather Jacket (Recommended: Aviatrix Biker Jacket)
  - o Gray Wind Breaker (Recommended: WIV Men's Bomber)
- Shoes
  - o Basic Color Athletic Shoes (Recommended: Nike Flyknit Roshe)
  - o Accent Color Athletic Shoes (Recommended: Nike Revolution 4)
  - o Black Boots (Recommended: La Milano Leather Dress Boots)
  - o Brown Boots (Recommended: Globalwin Winter Combat Boots)
- Accessories
  - o Silver Watch (Recommended: Invicta 'Speedway' Quartz Watch)
  - o Silver Necklace (Recommended: Silver Alloy Dog Tags)
  - o Reversible Belt (Recommended: Bulliant Reversible Belt)

With just the items listed above, you will have a wardrobe that is literally 90% complete, and that looks better than 90% of guys. If you want to shell out some extra money, you can, but I specifically chose the most inexpensive options I could find while still maintaining quality.

In general, you want to have these items, because they're very easy to match without thinking too much. You could basically grab any one piece from the categories in the above list, then throw them all together, and there's a 99% chance it will look good.

Going out and you're in a hurry? Just grab a white t-shirt, some dark denim jeans, a black leather jacket, the black boots, throw on a watch and necklace, and you're done.

See how simple it is? That list is specifically made to be a foundation for any guy's wardrobe – and anything else you want to buy on top of it is just gravy.

Lastly, let's talk about congruence. The goal of your style should be to maintain congruence. In other words, if you're a conservative Christian, wearing a "Misfits" punk rock t-shirt might not be the best fit. If you're a pot-smoking college dropout, though? It's perfect.

Keep in mind that there are a few separate "looks" that most men go for, that women generally react to favorably. Take, for example, the picture below. This is the "rugged man" look, that women generally go crazy over.

Do you notice how they're all congruent? All of them are basically following the same style: a nice pair of jeans, a basic color T-shirt, and a cool leather jacket. The shoes match, the accessories match, and the images are congruent.

Now, let's take a look at another look which I've dubbed the "urban minimalist" look. This is characterized by a minimalist approach to style, with base colors, and a few cool accessories.

Again, do you notice how it's congruent? Nothing is out of place. None of those guys are wearing a gigantic necklace with a bunch of crazy gems and sparkling jewels on it, like they're a rapper or something. They aren't wearing anything that "pops" too much, and it's just a bunch of nice, sleek, basic colors.

That's a great look to go for. In fact, it makes up a lot of my style. Still, though, I like to have a little bit more "edge" and "color accent" than these images, which is why I'll typically throw in some red shoes, an earring, or maybe a "peacocking" accessory.

As a man, one of the fastest and easiest things you can do to improve your physical attractiveness, is to simply add some edge to your style. When you add edginess to your style, you stand out, and show women that you're not afraid to stand out. This indirectly displays a lot of confidence, while simultaneously drawing more attention to you.

Lastly, let's take a look at the "gym style" that I often wear to the gym. I used to be against this, because I figured I was at the gym to work out and not to look good, but after my workouts I'll sometimes do day game with a pump, and I like looking stylish while I'm doing it.

Notice how it's all congruent. Nobody is wearing jeans to the gym with a tank top – that would just look strange. They're not wearing a shiny silver watch either, because nobody wears a shiny silver watch to the gym. It's all congruent with the look they're going for.

Not to beat a dead horse, but again, this is the biggest thing to master: congruence. You want your image to be congruent with who you are as a person. Nothing more, nothing less.

Now, I know what you're thinking:

> *"But Jon, if I normally wear sweat-stained undershirts and cheap sweatpants, isn't THAT what's congruent with who I am? Shouldn't I wear those things?"*

The answer, of course, is a resounding NO! It's "congruent" with your beta male, uneducated, failing-with-women self, not your alpha male self. Any change in your behaviors and habits is going to feel "incongruent" at first. This is normal. Eventually, however, it will become a part of your personality, and you will grow to love it.

Good Hygiene

Next, there's good hygiene. This will be a very short section, because there isn't much to talk about here. That being said, there's still three things I want to cover:

1. Soap
2. Deodorant
3. Cologne

When used in conjunction, these three things are actually a lot more powerful than you might think. Studies have shown that women have a very acute sense of smell (much more acute than men), and they can literally smell when a man has high testosterone.

That's why I personally LOVE using pheromone soap, which is specially formulated to make you smell like a high testosterone alpha male. Tactical Soap, which I stand behind and recommend 100%, loads their soap up with pheromones such as androstenone, which literally turns women on when they smell it.

I'm not even exaggerating, either. I've had girls give me a hug, and stick their nose into my armpit, and yell out: "Oh my God, you smell amazing!" It feels incredible knowing that girls are addicted to my "scent" and they always try to steal my hoodies afterward so they can smell it all day long while they wear it.

The next thing you want to do is get the right deodorant. Personally, I'm not too picky when it comes to deodorant. I just think it's important to use it. I prefer Speed Stick Ocean Surf, because it smells great and gets the job done. I've been using it for years and have never had a bad experience. Like I said, your deodorant isn't that important – it's not really meant to create a sexy smell, but rather STOP a sweaty, gross smell.

Lastly, is your cologne – and trust me, you do not want to skimp on this one. As I said before, studies have shown that women have a powerful sense of smell, and they can pick up on a lot that you might not notice.

With that in mind, I recommend you read the article which I wrote several years ago, on the sexiest colognes I've found (split tested from literally dozens). Google "Masculine Development best colognes for men" to find it.

Out of everything that I've tested, I've found that these three colognes work the best:

1. Cool Water by Davidoff
2. Very Sexy For Him 2 by Victoria's Secret
3. Roadster by Cartier

Investing in a good cologne doesn't have to be expensive – the ones listed above will only run you about $3 per month. I personally wear one of those three colognes everywhere I go, and girls always compliment me on them.

To apply it correctly, just put a spritz on your neck, a spritz on your chest, and then put a spritz on your wrist. Rub your wrists together, so the scent gets onto both wrists. I do this every day after I shower, and again right before I go out to the clubs. It works like a charm.

In addition to these three things, I also recommend you follow a good skincare routine. I personally use Treactive products for my face, and I've found that they work quite well.

I have naturally oil and acne-prone skin, so I use the following once a day:

- Acne Eliminating Face Cleanser
- Acne Eliminating Toner
- Acne Eliminating Moisturizer

Anyone who knows anything about a skincare routine will tell you that there's three basic components: the cleanser, the toner, and the moisturizer.

The cleanser gets rid of any dirt and oil that's on your skin, while also removing dead skin cells. The toner closes your pores, so that dirt can't get in as easily. The moisturizer ensures your skin stays wrinkle-free, and it also helps to cut down on flakes and acne.

Like I said, I personally use these Treactive products daily, and have been doing so for about 8 months now. I've found that these products work better than anything else I've used so far, but depending on your skin, you might want to try something else. Take it for what it's worth!

Part 3: Game

"Attract, comfort, seduce."
-Mystery, AKA Erik Von Markovik

"It's not lying, it's flirting."
-Neil Strauss, *The Game*

Executive Summary

Game is simply your ability to meet, attract, and sleep with women. While there is obviously more nuance than this, this is the essential purpose of game. There are different types of game, which should be employed under different circumstances, but make no mistake. They are all intended to spike a woman's emotions, turn her on, and make her sexually attracted to you.

At first, these concepts may feel "unnatural" or "manipulative." This is normal. You're evolving into a different person – one who succeeds with women – so of course, it's going to feel strange at first. Over time, however, you will naturally begin to attract women, by subconsciously internalizing the techniques and concepts discussed throughout this book.

The #1 most important thing, when it comes to game, is making her feel. Women want to feel the full range of emotions when they're with you: jealousy, anger, excitement, arousal, love, hate, curiosity, and intrigue. Emotions are exciting, and boredom is death.

There are four types of game which will be discussed in this chapter. The first, is "Demonstrating Higher Value," or DHV for short. This leverages a woman's natural hypergamy by demonstrating to her that you're higher up on the food chain than she is.

The second type of game, is spiking her emotions. This is extremely effective in the short-run, but can be challenging to keep up in the long-run. This type of game is exactly what it sounds like. You say things, do things, and act in a certain way, to make her FEEL.

Third, is "hoop theory" or getting her qualifying. This is a psychological hack which encourages women to do your own seduction work for you, and it hinges upon a powerful set of subconscious rules. Effectively, it's getting her to prove that she's "worthy" of dating you.

Lastly, is dread game. This type of game is phenomenal for ensuring loyalty in the longer term, as it hinges upon a woman's fear of you finding another woman. When a woman understands that you're a high-value man who could easily find another woman in a heartbeat, she will naturally become more attracted to you.

I understand that some of these concepts may sound manipulative, but I don't make the rules, I just state the facts – and these are the facts. Whether women want to admit this or not, these things work... and I've got a notch count in the triple digits to show it.

Chapter 9. What is Game?

Put simply, "game" is your ability to meet, attract, and sleep with high-quality women. Of course, many other writers have come up with long, convoluted definitions of "game," but really that's all it comes down to.

Game is unique in that it is primarily focused on the WOMAN. Optimizing things such as your lifestyle, your appearance, and your energy will all certainly make women far more attracted to you, but they're focused on YOU – not HER.

With game, however, it is 100% focused on her, in the moment. Game is an active process (most of the time, but I'll elaborate more on that later). It is not something you can do sitting around, although when you get really good, you will have a "residual" effect from your game.

Primarily, the goal of game is to get a woman into a "buying state" in which she's ready, wanting, and willing to have sex with you. This typically entails of spiking her emotions...

The Master Key of Game

The biggest, most important thing to focus on in "game" is how she FEELS. I don't give a damn about what she "thinks" because it doesn't matter. When it comes to attraction, all that matters is how you make her FEEL. This is Female Psychology 101.

She could THINK you're a dick, a loser, and a total scumbag, but if you make her FEEL excitement and validation when she's around you, then she will fall in love with you.

Half of the time, it doesn't even matter which emotions you make her feel. Of course, it's always better to make her feel the "good" emotions, but sometimes feeling the "bad" ones is better than feeling nothing.

In fact, as you go through your life and date different types of women, you will be able to identify a very specific type: the drama queen. These girls THRIVE off of negative emotions, and even if they act as if they want you to be a good boy and behave, they really get off on you being a dick and fucking other girls.

Now, of course, not all girls are like this. Many girls who have a high level of self-esteem will not tolerate you insulting them. That being said, there is a small subset of women (probably 10%) who likes being with the asshole. I don't recommend you date these girls, because they will fuck your life up if you let them. With that in mind, many of them are fun to date and sleep with for a short time.

Roller Coaster of Emotions

When a woman starts to date you, she typically wants the full range of emotions. She wants to feel jealousy, knowing that you might be off fucking other girls. Women will never admit this, sometimes even to themselves, but it EXCITES them knowing that you're off fucking other girls.

They enjoy the chase – ESPECIALLY the high-quality women. Nothing disgusts them more than a guy who is too quick to settle down. This is not masculine energy – masculine energy wants to be free, and it wants to dominate the world. Again, think of a charging bull.

Does a charging bull, or a soaring eagle want to be tied down and domesticated? Of course not. It wants to roam free – free to do whatever it wants. This is the ever-elusive "masculine energy" that women are inexorably drawn to.

Feminine energy wants to "trap," and it wants to "tame." This is why women will always chase what they cannot have, and it's why there is nothing more satisfying to a woman than when she can tame an alpha male, through the sheer intuition and allure of her feminine energy.

Nothing validates a woman more, than "turning" the player, or the fuck boy, into a genuinely nice guy. Nothing is more rewarding, fulfilling, and enjoyable to a woman, than the back-and-forth process of taming and capturing a man's wild, primal energy, and making him her own.

Chapter 10. Types of Game

With this in mind, let's talk about the different types of game. Yes, that's right – there are many kinds of game. As I said previously, however, they are all hinged on one simple thing: making women feel emotions.

Every type of game is meant to make her feel; jealousy, desire, excitement, arousal, fear, and joy. Women want the full experience. So, give it to them.

Demonstrating Higher Value (DHV)

One powerful form of game that can be used in any situation, is "DHV game," short for "Demonstrating Higher Value" game. This type of game leverages female hypergamy, and is specifically meant to make her view you as "higher up" on the hierarchy than she is.

When a man subtly mentions the fact that he's a DJ at some cool, trendy night club? That's demonstrating higher value. When a man talks about how he's traveled the world, and been to all the places she wants to be? That's demonstrating higher value.

When a man talks about how he has more Instagram followers than she does? That's demonstrating higher value. When he's acting indifferent, as if she's not pretty enough for him? That as well, is demonstrating higher value.

You can demonstrate higher value in many different ways, but the best "way" to do it, is to not actually try to do it at all.

Girls are very attuned to when a man tries to brag to turn her on. Never brag to a girl, because it comes off as very "try hard" and funny enough, actually has the opposite effect. What does bragging to a girl sub-communicate to her? That you're trying to impress her, AKA that you're lower value, and trying to work your way up.

Instead, I recommend just subtly dropping a few things out there every now and then, if you can. They should be relevant to HER wants and needs, however. In other words, you want to be the man who's experienced in the world she wants to be in.

For example, say that she wants to be a famous actress. Then, she meets a man who's been in the acting industry for the past 15 years, and who's had several small hits. This man would be the epitome of DHV for her, because he's literally 15 years more "higher value" than her in the exact thing she wants to succeed at.

Take another example, in which a young girl goes clubbing a lot. If you're a DJ, a promoter, or even a bouncer, this means you have more "value" and more "power" in this world than she does, and by subtly communicating this, she will become more attracted to you.

Now, I know exactly what you're thinking:

"But Jon, what if I'm too young and inexperienced to have higher value than her? I'm only [XYZ age] and don't have anything to brag about. How do I get her then?"

By fully believing and internalizing that you're "cooler" than she is. I know this may sound stupid, but as we've said a billion times before, when you fully believe something to be true, women will pick up on your confidence and start to believe you are higher value, too.

There are a few ways you can do this, but ultimately, it all comes down to your frame. If you believe that you're cooler than her, higher value than her, and have more options than her, it doesn't really matter if you actually DO have these things or not.

She will pick up on your confidence, and naturally become more attracted to you.

Spiking Her Emotions

Perhaps the most powerful type of "game" is simply spiking her emotions. There are guys out there, who have literally dedicated their entire lives to spiking a girl's emotions. Think of a man such as Dan Bilzerian or Hugh Hefner. They literally live in giant mansions with tons of weed, hot tubs, stripper poles, foam cannons, and other cool shit, SPECIFICALLY to get girls excited.

When a woman is excited, and her emotions are running high, she will do almost anything with you. Even if she didn't want to do that exact same thing 15 minutes earlier, she will often change her mind, because she thinks with her FEELINGS, not her THOUGHTS.

In other words, if something feels good, and it "feels right" to a woman, then in her world, it is. Many men can't understand this, because we are logical creatures. We analyze everything, and we create these great, giant mental frameworks to deconstruct the world, which is very masculine... and it's very important.

But to the feminine, emotions are all that matters. Something is "wrong" if it feels wrong, and something is "right" if it feels right. Again, this is why you see women denouncing "players" and "fuckboys" one second, but after 15 minutes of conversation with them, they're in love.

Why? Because in those 15 minutes, her brain shifted gears. Due to his "game", she went from being in a logical, analytical mindset, to an emotional, and feeling mindset. This is the master key to game, really – getting her to feel emotions.

So, with that in mind, how do you spike her emotions? There are a few ways to do so, but the first thing you must understand is the Law of State Transference.

According to the "Law of State Transference," whatever you feel, she will eventually feel. Etch this law into your fucking forehead, because it's the primal cause of game.

Have you ever wondered why when you're in a good mood, women seem to magically open up to you more? They're more receptive, happier around you, and flirt with you more. Even men, who might typically be more reserved, are friendlier around you.

Why is this? It's due to the Law of State Transference. Whatever you feel, others will eventually feel. To elaborate a little bit more, and create a lengthier version: "Whatever the _highest confidence person_ feels, everyone else will eventually feel."

In other words, whoever holds the strongest frame, will eventually begin to influence other peoples' frames. This is why it's so important that you learn to generate good emotions from within, because if you can do this, a whole new world of social success will open up to you.

So, with this in mind, when you're trying to spike a girl's emotions, the most important thing is that you FEEL the same feeling you want her to feel. For example, last night I was with a girl, and we were flirting, cuddling, and making out a bit. I then grabbed her by the neck, pulled her hair, asked: "Do you like that?" in a very dominant, assertive way. She moaned and said: "Yes, Daddy."

Now, why did this work? If some other guy with less experience in game had tried this, he would have likely been yelled at and kicked out of her house. So why did it work with me? Because I understood a few things.

First, I understood that her emotions were sufficiently spiked. She was sufficiently turned on and aroused for me to do this. Second, I realized that she viewed me as "cool" and "high value," because I am naturally good at holding this frame. Third, I understood that if I get aroused *while I'm doing it,* she will get aroused while I'm doing it as well.

I know it's kind of a random (and personal) example, but it illustrates this fact perfectly. If you are in a good mood, and you are filled with arousal, joy, and excitement, she will likely feel the same emotions as you.

Have you ever had a friend who was just so upbeat that it was infectious? Or perhaps a teacher who was so passionate about the subject material, that you couldn't help but be enrapt in it? This is the Law of State Transference at work.

It's also why being genuine, and vulnerable is so effective. When you fully acknowledge who you are, without any filters or masks, other people can sense it. They then let their guard down, and get drawn into your world. If you're more confident in who you truly are then they are, then they will naturally follow your lead.

A common problem that many men have is the "Nice Guy Syndrome," which is basically the inability to spike her emotions. Nice Guys™ are fundamentally afraid of saying anything that will offend her, so they just shower her in compliments and gifts, hoping to get laid. As I've discussed before, women find nice guys repulsive, because they're not genuine.

With this in mind, here's a good exercise to start destroying your "nice guy" persona. The next time you go out, immediately and automatically disagree with EVERYTHING she says.

If she says "I'm from DC!" tell her: "I fucking HATE DC! Everyone is such a DICK there!"

Now, of course, say it with a smile. You don't want to start an open confrontation, but by doing this, you will be learning a valuable lesson: it's okay to disagree.

In fact, what you'll start to notice is that, if your frame is strong, she will actually AGREE with you. Whenever I do this exercise to show students in the field, I always say the following:

> *"You're from [XYZ]? Oh my God, I fucking HATE that place! Everyone is such a dick there! I was literally there the other day, driving around, and I asked the guy next to me where the nearest gas station was. He literally just STARED at me, and ROLLED UP HIS WINDOW! Like without even breaking eye contact!"*

I typically get responses like: *"HAHA! Okay, okay that's true, people can be mean there,"* or "oh my God, I'm so sorry haha! That's so mean of them to do!!!"

Again, what does this illustrate? Two things:

1. It's okay to disagree with her (AKA to break your Nice Guy syndrome)
2. She will typically agree if you have the stronger frame

Now, will you get some girls who are just random bitches, and who will blow you out? Of course, you will. That's part of the game. But we're men. We put up with it. All it takes is one "yes" to make your night spectacular... and to me, that's worth a thousand "no's."

Here are some other miscellaneous ways to spike her emotions. I use all of them together in my game:

1. Telling Stories
2. Using A Good Opener
3. Dancing With Her
4. Escalating On Her Physically
5. Utilize Your Environment

Telling stories is a great way to spike her emotions, but you have to do it with confidence and assertiveness – like you've told it 10,000 times and know exactly what you're doing. Learning to tell stories is a great skill to have as well, because in order to get good at it, you have to be good at reading the listeners' facial expressions, and calibrating accordingly.

In addition to this, telling stories that demonstrate higher value are great. I've got a ton of stories that I tell girls (if the subject comes up, of course), that consistently demonstrate higher value. Stories about how I used to be a huge drug dealer (disclaimer: not true), about how I have friends who throw crazy parties, and about how I have a lot of pre-selection.

A good story should do four main things:

1. Spike her existing emotions
2. Demonstrate higher value
3. Show pre-selection
4. Build comfort

If you can come up with a story that does all four of these, girls will be eating out of the palm of your hands. I don't necessarily advise memorizing "canned stories" like other pickup artists talk about, but if you need to memorize some fake stories to improve your game, so be it. Just be sure to use them as TRAINING WHEELS, and not as the ultimate end goal.

For example, sometimes I'll tell the story about the first time I did cocaine (again, disclaimer: not true). Here's what that might look like:

I was at my buddy's beach house in Polly's Island (like a classier Myrtle Beach) for Spring Break, and he threw this HUGE party. It was crazy – we had a private section of the beach and everything, so we didn't have to worried about getting busted or shut down.

These two guys came down from New York City to party for a whole week, and they were LOADED with cocaine. I assume it was good shit too, since they got if from New York. Anyways, in the middle of the party, I ended up snorting lines off a girl's ass – her name was CiCi – and I got so hype and fired up, that I literally tore my shirt off and started flexing my muscles.

That whole week was insane. This one girl got really drunk, and we had to make sure none of the random guys there did anything to her, she was like throwing up and everything. We got her into a room where she could be safe, and I watched over her for a little bit until she got better... all in all it was a pretty crazy vacation.

Now – what does this story do? First off, it spikes her existing emotions. As I tell the story, I literally feel the emotions of adventure, fun, and excitement, so that they radiate off of me onto her. Second, it shows high value. The fact that I had access to a private beach house party, with a ton of cocaine, and sexy girls who I could snort it off of, is pretty high value.

Third, it shows pre-selection. The fact that there was a ton of other girls there, and that I snorted cocaine off of a girl's ass, shows that I have other girls who are sexually invested and interested in me. Fourth, it builds comfort – the fact that I watched after a girl when she was really drunk shows that I'm a "protector" and that I'm safe to be around.

Stories that do all four of these things are hard to come by, but if it makes you feel more confident, you can use that story that I just gave you. Hell, you can use my name if that makes you more confident, too. Introduce yourself as Jon Anthony for all I care.

Another way to spike a girl's emotions is to use a good opener. All good openers have enough emotional "hooks" to make her feel something:

- "You look like a Scorpio."
- "Did you see that chick fight outside? It was crazy."
- "Who cheats more: guys or girls?"

They might seem stupid, but that's the point. They're crazy, silly, and a little bit random, to get her intrigued and to make her start feeling things with you. That's the only goal of game, really – to make her FEEL things, and get her into an emotional, feminine state.

Dancing with her and escalating on her physically are also great ways to spike her emotions. You want to be careful with escalation, though. Too much escalation in public can kill the sexual tension, and before you know it, she won't want to come home with you. I recommend you keep the public displays of affection at a minimum, where kissing is the most you do.

Another great way to spike a girl's emotions is to simply use your environment. For example, I used to have a mini trampoline at my old place, just because when girls would come back, their eyes would grow wide and they would want to jump around on it.

There are a million different ways to spike a girl's emotions, you just have to get enough experience to start realizing how it's done. Again, remember that every variation of game is really just attempting to spike her emotions. Arousal, jealousy, anger, sadness, pity, joy, desire, depression, ecstasy, and longing – it doesn't matter what she feels, just so much that she feels.

As a quick side note, as well – only ever escalate and close on a HIGH NOTE.

In other words, the time to try to kiss her isn't after some long, drawn out silence. It's after you tell a funny joke, and she starts laughing hysterically. Always escalate on the high notes, and your close rate will literally triple overnight.

Getting Her Qualifying

Another tried and true type of game, is to simply get her qualifying. What this means is you want to get her jumping through YOUR hoops, not the other way around. Most guys go up to a girl and start qualifying right off the bat. They try to prove themselves, as if she's some divine goddess whose approval they need to earn.

This type of behavior is repulsive to women, because it's validation-seeking. As a man, you want to be the source of your own validation – again, this is masculine energy. You want to draw state and validation from within, not from without. As a man, you want her validation to be anchored to YOU, just as a little girl's validation is tied to her father's approval or disapproval.

While this may sound weird or strange, it's true. This is where the whole "daddy" kink comes from. When a girl is young, she derives approval from her father. When she does something good, he gives her a smile, or a pat on the head, or a big old hug. When she does something bad, he chastises her, corrects her firmly, or maybe gives her a spanking.

When a girl grows up, this imprint is still there – most men just can't fill it. It takes the right kind of man to get her qualifying, and she isn't going to let her guard down for just anyone. You need to show her that you're the right man, and that she can trust your guidance and leadership as a man. If you can do this, she will shower your world in love and light.

All spiritual talk aside, getting a girl qualifying is one of the most powerful ways to get her chasing. The best way to get a girl qualifying, in my opinion, is to simply know EXACTLY what you want from her. When you're 100% clear in your expectations, and you refuse to break your frame, she will naturally fall in line as she comes to trust and adore you.

Take some time to answer the following questions:

1. What does your perfect 10 look like? How tall is she? How much does she weigh? What color eyes does she have? What color hair? What is her body type? Be specific.
2. What is her personality like? Is she shy? Outgoing? Adventurous? Loyal? Again, be as specific as you possibly can.

When you take some time to create your "perfect 10," you'll start to naturally screen women for these characteristics. Even if you're talking to a girl who's absolutely beautiful, deep down you'll be asking yourself questions like: "Is she the type of girl who will be loyal to me? Is she going to bust my balls, or support me? What's her personality like?"

In addition to setting some ideals, you can also ask qualifying questions. Getting a girl to start qualifying herself to you is a bit of an art form, but once you get the hang of it, you'll begin to recognize how easy it is to do.

Here are a few qualifying questions you can ask to get her started:

1. What do you do for a living?
2. Are you spontaneous or are you a planner?
3. Do you like [X Band] or not?
4. You look like you were an emo in high school.

It doesn't really matter what you ask her or say to her. What matters is your response to HER response. Take, for example, the following conversation that I had with a girl last week. Look at how I ask innocent questions, but slowly start to get her qualifying herself to me:

> Jon: "What do you do for a living?"
> Girl: "I work for Deloitte! I'm an accountant."

105

Jon: "Oh, hmm. That's... cool, I guess."
Girl: "Haha, thanks, I mean it's alright."

Now, to most men, this looks like a completely normal conversation. But to those of you who've been in the field long enough, you can see the slight shift after my response to HER response.

Notice how I started off by asking her a regular, standard question that she probably gets asked all the time. "What do you do for a living?" How often do you think a girl gets asked something like that? All of the fucking time, of course.

So, what did she say? The canned response that she probably says to every other guy. "I work for Deloitte! I'm an accountant." Okay, cool – nothing special here. The MAGIC, however, is in how you respond to the way she ANSWERS your question.

What did I say in response? "Oh, hmm. That's... cool, I guess." Doesn't seem like a very special answer, does it? That's the whole point – game is supposed to be subtle. There are times where being obvious and flashy is fun, but ultimately, if it doesn't lead to a result, it's pointless.

Anyways – my response to her question sub-communicated a few powerful things:

1. I wasn't very impressed (which I wasn't, I think accounting is boring as fuck)
2. I'm not going to act impressed, because I'm not (AKA I'm being congruent)
3. I'm socially savvy enough to just be polite

Some guys when they first get into game, are too abrasive and not calibrated enough. In other words, they would've said something like: "Wow, that sucks." Admittedly, this can work well sometimes (as with anything in game, it's not the line, but how

106

you use it). But overall, politely conveying your lack of interest seemed like the best thing for me to do at the time.

So, what did she say in response? "Haha, thanks, I mean it's alright." Now, again – this doesn't seem like a particularly interesting comment, does it? But here's the key... notice the SLIGHT shift in her attitude towards her own job. Rather than saying something like: "Yeah, I love it!" she noticed that I wasn't impressed, and so started QUALIFYING herself to me, by slightly agreeing that it isn't the best job. "Haha, yeah, *I mean it's alright.*"

This is how subtle these things are sometimes, and this is how socially intelligent women are. They're literally attuned to the SLIGHTEST little shifts in conversation, emotion, body language, and facial expressions, to the point that it would absolutely blow your mind if you got to experience her reality for just a few short days.

This is what qualification usually looks like. It's her SLIGHTLY changing her responses to match whatever your frame is. It doesn't always have to be super extreme.

That being said, there are times where it WILL be extreme. I've had girls literally blurt out things like: "I'm REALLY good at sucking dick," when they're trying to get my attention. This is an extreme form of qualification, and it means you should take your shot... now.

Again, though – as with everything in game, there is a flipside. Sometimes, especially if you're in public, you want to MINIMIZE the overt and obvious signs of qualification, because her female friends will notice that she's emotional and horny, and will come in to cock block you. It's always best to be smooth, subtle, and cool, and fly under the radar. If you're a newbie though, just take what you can get. Don't worry about being subtle quite yet – just get experience.

Dread Game

Next up, there's dread game. This type of game is great AFTER you've already slept with a girl, and are interested in keeping her around. It isn't that effective at getting girls interested in you initially, but man is it great for getting your girlfriend to crave you perpetually.

The basic premise behind dread game is simple: you demonstrate an abundance of women, and such high pre-selection, that she's always "dreading" that you'll go off and shack up with some younger, prettier, perkier girl than her.

As I mentioned before, pre-selection is a very powerful thing. While women will never admit it, secretly, it EXCITES them when other women want you. It requires a lot of balancing to keep a girl around, particularly between the following two things:

1. Her belief that you have tons of other girls who want you
2. Her belief that you're loyal and willing to stick around

If you emphasize one of these too much, and not enough of the other, bad things happen. If a girl thinks you will be 100% loyal, but she can tell that no other girls are interested in you, then she will naturally start to believe you aren't worth keeping. After all, if no other girls want to have sex with you, then why should she?

If you emphasize the fact that you have tons of other girls around who WANT you too much, however, she might be afraid that she won't stand a chance, and she won't even bother trying to lock you down. This is why, in my opinion, combining sheer sexuality and masculinity with being GENUINE, is one of the most powerful ways to attract a woman.

If you come off as a total alpha male, she will grow attracted to you immensely. That isn't what will keep her around, though – this will get her interested... at first. What will keep her around is your alpha male energy COMBINED with you showing her who you truly are, and developing an emotional, spiritual, and sexual connection with her.

When she sees that you have all of these other girls, but you open up to HER, she will feel incredibly validated as a woman. She will feel special, and privileged to know who you truly are. After all, you could have opened up to any of those other girls – but you chose her. This is the best way to secure a long-term partner: not from scarcity, but from abundance.

Now, of course, I know what you're thinking (as usual):

> *"But Jon, isn't it manipulative for me to do this? I don't want her to be afraid I'm going to leave her! I love her, and I want to stay with her for the rest of my life!"*

Well, let me ask you a question, then, in response. If you love her, do you not want her to feel VALIDATED as a woman? While she may SAY that she wants you to cut off all contact with your female friends, and give her 100% of your attention, deep down, she wants you to say no.

Deep down, the best way to validate your woman, is to make it very clear that you have other options, but that you chose her. Knowing that an alpha male chose HER, because he genuinely loves her, is the most incredible feeling for a woman. It will set her soul on fire, and electrify her very being. She will wake up craving your love, and go to sleep thinking about you.

I know it might be hard to except, but plenty of men learn the hard way. In fact, I would like to make a prediction right now... you're going to learn the hard way yourself. You're going to get into a relationship with a girl. It's going to start off great. You're going to have tons of sex all the time, and she's going to tell you to stop talking to those other girls, and to stop hanging out with all of your female friends.

...and, like a fool, you're going to do it. You're going to do it, thinking that she's going to fall in love with you even more, but instead, you're going to notice something happen: she's going to fall out of love with you. She isn't going to have sex with you as often, and when she does, it's going to just be "maintenance sex," not the passionate, wild, sweaty sex you once had.

Over time, you're going to grow confused. In a desperate attempt to regain her former feelings for you, you're going to start qualifying yourself to her, changing your habits, and following her orders. She will throw you some pity sex every now and then as a reward, but it will never be the same as it first was.

Eventually, she will decide to break up with you. "You're just not the man I fell in love with," she'll say. "I don't feel the same way about you that I used to," she'll tell you. "What can I do to make it better?" you'll ask. "What can I do to change that?" you'll beg. But, the fact remains, that you lost your mojo. The spark is dead, and she will move on.

Okay – if that sounds oddly familiar to you, let me break down why this happens. When a girl first gets into a relationship with you, she will begin to test you. Her feminine energy wants to know that you are a solid foundation; a rock that she can set herself upon safely. She wants to know that she can trust you, and that you are a true alpha male, who can lead by example.

She will start to say things like: "I wish you would stop spending so much time at the gym and just spend time with me," or "Why do you talk to all those other girls? Am I not good enough?" She will say these things in an attempt to throw you off your purpose. Of course, she doesn't know it – but it's real, and it's happening to her and you.

If you refuse to cave in, she may grow angry at first, but in the same way that a little girl grows angry at her father for setting boundaries. Over time, she will grow to love and accept her father, and she will realize that these boundaries make her feel safe. The same can be said about our relationship example here. She may grow angry with you at first, but over time, she will begin to accept that you are an alpha male who is on his purpose in life.

If she continues to bother you for more attention, and continues to bug you over your female friends, one of two things is probably wrong:

1. You're not giving her enough attention
2. She has low self-esteem

Either you're not giving her enough attention, so that she knows these other girls aren't necessarily a threat, or she simply has low self-esteem and will never be satisfied with any man who she finds. If it's the latter, unfortunately, you need to break it off.

A high self-esteem woman will be turned on by the fact that you have other girls in your life. I've said it before, and I'll say it again. Women will never admit this, but it secretly excites them, knowing that you have other women who want you.

Let me tell you a success story about a recent coaching client of mine...

About a month ago, I got a request for a coaching call. The man told me a very common story – one that I hear all of the time. He said that the passion just wasn't there in his relationship anymore, and that him and his wife rarely ever had sex.

I told him to start using "dread game," and making it IMPLICITLY clear that you have other women interested in you. I don't care what it takes – mention the girls at work, mention how a girl complimented you at the gym, whatever. Just start implying that other girls want you.

Within literally a single week, he told me that she "dropped onto her knees" and started sucking his cock. While many men

111

might find it hard to believe this, it's true – when women sense that other women want you, it secretly arouses and excites them.

This is the power of dread game.

Part 4: Meeting Women

"Get over your inhibitions and approach as many sets as you can. A guy that does 100 in a day will close more and learn more than someone that does not."

-Richard LaRuina

"Approach anxiety is something everyone new to game has to deal with. If you don't deal with that discomfort, you're never going to get better with women."

-Adam Lyons

Executive Summary

In short, this part deals with the mechanics of actually meeting women, and is divided into two main sections. The first section is on where to meet women, and the second section is on how to meet women. Both are extremely important to understand and implement into your life.

There are five main categories of where to meet women, each with their own distinct benefits and drawbacks. The first is night game. This is simply meeting girls out during the night, at bars, nightclubs, and on at parties. The benefits of this are that you can approach many girls in a single night, gain a lot of experience quickly, and the environment is typically much more sexualized than during the day. The drawbacks are dealing with drunk people and encountering lots of drama.

The second is day game. Day game is meeting girls during the day, at malls, at coffee shops, and on your way to work. The benefits of day game are that you can do it anywhere and anytime, and you will often meet a much higher quality of woman. The drawbacks are that it's limited in its ability to actually teach you game, because during the day, pretty girls are far and few between (unless you live in a city like New York, Las Vegas, or a college town).

The third is social circle game. This is how most men meet their girlfriends – through their social circle. The benefits of this are that once you know how, you can make your social circle work for you. Women in your social circle are also more attracted to you, simply because you have more social proof than a random person they've never met. The drawbacks are that it's quite limited, and you may only meet 1-2 new girls a month through this method.

The fourth, is online dating – one of my favorites. This way of meeting women employs dating applications such as Tinder and Bumble, to screen a wide variety of women at once, and end up with a handful of qualified candidates. The benefits are that it's quick, easy, and cheap, and you're often dealing with vast quantities of women. The drawbacks, are that with online dating, looks play a much more significant role, and flakiness is a lot higher.

Lastly, the fifth type is through social media. This is a unique way of meeting women that is still evolving, but I believe it deserves a thorough examination. The benefits of this type of game are that, if you can use it correctly, you will have an abundance of women, and retaining women will be much easier. The drawbacks, however, are that most men cannot even compete in this sphere.

The second topic "Part 4" deals with, is how to meet women using the "OSSE" Framework I've created. This comes down to open, social hook point, sexual hook point, and extraction. The open is your opener – it's what you say to open the set. Once you open the set, you will move onto the social hook point, which is where she engages you in conversation.

Next, is the sexual hook point – where she begins to engage with you in a sexual, flirtatious manner. Then, is the extraction – where you can get her to a location that sex can occur. An experienced player knows how to effortlessly and easily transition from "open" to "extraction," and this is primarily what this section will be dealing with.

Chapter 11. Where to Meet Women

Now that you know more about how attraction works, let's talk about the actual nuts and bolts of meeting women. Here's where the rubber really meets the road. You can know all about masculine energy, being an alpha male, shit tests, and attraction, but if you don't actually know WHERE to go and HOW To use it, all of that knowledge is pointless.

That's what this section is for. In Part 4, I will discuss the specifics on how to meet women. We will discuss where to meet them, how to approach them, how to escalate on them, and everything else you need to know in order to get a steady influx of new women into your life.

So, with this in mind, let's jump right to it. There are five fundamental ways to meet new girls:

1. Night Game
2. Day Game
3. Social Circle
4. Online Dating
5. Social Media

Each one of these has its own unique benefits and drawbacks, but they all work best when used in conjunction with each other. That's why I recommend guys get a healthy taste of each kind, so that they can not only get more experience, but develop their own unique style of game.

Night Game

Ah, night game – the pickup artist's playing field. While much of the advice in the manosphere can be used in any situation, most of it is tailored towards night game. Things that work really well in night game will often work TERRIBLY under other conditions, so it's important to be aware of this distinction.

As I said before, every style of pickup has its own unique pros and cons. That being said, I still think that night game is by far the best way to learn game, period.

Here are the benefits of night game:

- There's extremely high volume
- Girls are more open to being approached
- Most girls are open to sleeping with the *right guy*
- People are in the socializing mode

Conversely, here are the drawbacks of night game:

- You'll have to deal with more bitchy girls
- Friends are notorious for cock-blocking
- Most of the girls are not LTR material

As I said previously, night game is by far the best way to learn game, hands down. The reason being that in no other context can you gain so many new reference experiences in such a short amount of time.

If you're trying to go through your social circle, for example, maybe you'll be able to meet two new girls a week. This adds up to about 104 girls a year.

With night game, however? You can literally talk to that many girls from just a week of going out. Hell, if you really wanted to push it, you could probably meet 104 new girls in a single NIGHT.

This is why night game is so powerful. It allows you to gain a massive amount of experience in such a short period of time, so that you can learn the social skills necessary to succeed with women. I recommend every man go through a period of at least half a year, where he goes out to nightclubs, bars, and other nighttime venues, at least 4x per week. This is also known as having an "immersion phase" for game.

Doing this will solidify your social skills, and present you with enough new experiences, so that you can start using these same skills in your social circle with ease.

Now, as I said, there are drawbacks to night game. One of the most significant drawbacks is that you'll meet all kinds of weird, drunk, and sometimes clinically insane people. Guys will try to start fights with you over stupid shit. Drunk girls will bitch at you for no reason. This is all part of the game – don't take it personally, because it isn't personal.

The main things to focus on for a successful "night game" session are:

- Speaking LOUDLY
- Approaching constantly
- Getting into "state"
- Staying SOBER
- Spiking emotions and buying temperature

If you can do these things properly, there is an incredibly high likelihood that you will pull. If you also adhere to the advice given on style, fitness, hygiene, grooming, and alpha male characteristics, the chance that you'll pull is probably between 50-90% per night depending on your skill level and previous experience.

First, speak loudly. Then, speak twice as loud. Seriously. When you go out, and the music is pounding, and everyone is drunk and chatting around, you need to talk LOUDLY for her to hear you properly. If you try to open her, and the first thing she says is: "WHAT?" you've already lost the set.

Second, approach constantly. Don't lose momentum. If you're in set with a girl and she seems to like you, and you have chemistry, make a commitment to focus on her and try to pull her (which will be addressed under the "How to Meet Women" chapter). If you get blown out, immediately open another set. Don't dick around on your phone, don't buy a drink, and don't get lost in your head. Stay present and open the next set.

Third, focus on getting into state. There's generally three parts of the night. Each part has its own unique characteristics, and you should adjust your game style slightly to fit the different parts of the night.

Here are the three parts of the night:

- Part 1 (9pm – 11pm)
- Part 2 (11pm – 2am)
- Part 3 (2am onwards)

The first part is from 9pm to about 11pm. This is when everyone is still unwinding and getting in the social mode. Focus on just chatting people up and being social, to get in state. Then, from 11pm to around 2am is the second part of the night. This is when things are getting more sexual. Focus on trying to close, spiking her buying temperature, and isolating (again this will be covered later).

Then, the last part of the night, is from around 2am onwards. I call this the "horny and confused" stage. Here, girls have been getting hit on all night, and they are horny because of it. They don't know why that "hot guy" from an hour ago didn't take them home, because, in girl land, they don't understand that game doesn't come naturally for most men.

For this part of the night, focus on being FRIENDLY and NOT being too sexually aggressive. You want to come across as friendly, while still maintaining a sexual vibe, but not being outright sexual. Girls will be screening pretty hard during this time of the night, as their state will start to crash. That being said, this

119

is also the "dirty 30," because about 30% of your lays will come from this last part of the night.

Another important note is to stay sober. Do not drink when you go out to learn game. Would you go to a class on computer coding drunk? Of course not. So why would you get drunk when you're trying to stay sharp and learn social skills? It might be difficult _at first_, but what you'll find is that, while people who drink get in state fast, they also crash fast, and get sloppy and stupid fast. It's better to be a "slow burner" and warm up over the course of the night.

Lastly, the main things to focus on during night game are spiking a woman's emotions and being aware of her buying temperature. Because of the chaotic nature of night game, you can get away with saying a lot more and doing a lot more than anywhere else. Using some of the tips I gave you before to spike her emotions will work well here.

Don't forget to focus on her buying temperature, either. I will talk more about this under the "How to Meet Women" chapter, but for now, understand that all women need to get "warmed up" before they're ready to have sex. Pay close attention to the girls you're talking to, and ask yourself if she's ready to hook up or not. Be lean, mean, and efficient.

Day Game

Next, there's day game. This is arguably my favorite type, for a few reasons. First off, day game is something you can do anywhere you go. Unlike night game, you don't really have to plan it – instead, it just happens. If you're out at the store, and you see a pretty girl, it can be extremely efficient and practical to just get her number then and there.

Day game is a little bit different in night game, in that with night game, you can get away with being a lot more sexually aggressive and obnoxious. With day game however, since there's no blaring music, alcohol, or deafening crowds talking around, it's wise to be a little bit more reserved. Still speak clearly and loudly of course, but keep it in mind.

Here are the pros of day game:

- You can do it anywhere
- The girls are often better LTR material
- Just approaching clearly shows your intent
- You can do it on your own time

Here are the cons of day game:

- Pretty girls are often few and far between
- Getting "instant lays" are a lot more difficult

Overall, I'm a not the biggest fan of day game, but I do think it's an important skillset to have. The most significant difference between day game and night game is that during the night, you can get away with having some weird personality quirks. You can get away with being a little bit weird, uncalibrated, anxious, and/or pushy.

During the day, however, it's a lot harder to do this. During the day, girls will be a lot more tuned into if you're "creepy" or "needy" or "weird" or not. In my experience, the most important thing during day game is to be slightly flirtatious, but not overly sexual.

I personally prefer to use day game as a _supplement_ to my regular night game sessions. When you master night game, day game typically becomes much easier.

The reason why is because in night game, you'll encounter so much more bullshit: her friends trying to cockblock you, angry ex-boyfriends, loud music, and whatever else. So once day game rolls around, it's like turning the "difficulty level" down a few notches.

The main things to focus on for day game are the following:

- Use it as a supplement to regular night game sessions
- Focus on being friendly, upbeat, and social
- Try being less sexual, although don't be afraid to escalate
- Focus on getting numbers and leads for later dates

In my opinion, day game is best for obtaining high-quality numbers. With night game, you'll get a lot of numbers, but they'll be flaky. With day game, however, you'll get fewer numbers, but the girls who give them to you will typically be less flaky and higher quality.

They'll also tend to remember you more. Girls get approached all the time at night clubs and bars, but when she's at the mall? It doesn't happen that often. You'll make a much stronger impression, and she'll be much more inclined to remember you.

Social Circle Game

There's a term that's been floating around the pickup community lately called "social circle game" which I believe is a little bit of a misnomer. That being said, it is a very powerful concept once you clarify some of the subtler points.

The whole goal of social circle game is to create a unique and complex ecosystem within your life, that nourishes and supports you. Ideally, you should have a lot of friends in powerful places, who invite you to cool events and genuinely care about your life.

The best way to think about your friends and family is by using what I've dubbed the "Lion's Circle." I believe we can learn a lot from nature, in all of its profound, ancestral wisdom, and this is the best framework for understanding how to categorize your relationships that I've come across so far.

Every lion in the wild has three categories of friends:

- The Harem
- The Tribe
- The Pack

Lions in the harem are great for partying and having fun, but not much else. These are the guys in your life who are fun to hang around, but aren't really "close friends." They're the people from work you go out and get drinks with, the friends who you take out to go clubbing, and the girls you fuck every now and then.

Then, there's the tribe – this is your group of close friends. These are the people you regularly talk to, and who you go deep with. They're the people who you can rely on in a bind, and who are willing to have your back if push comes to shove.

Then, however, there's the PACK. These are the motherfuckers you link up with and will ride with until you die. These are the people who you confide in, who you TRULY confide in. The pack never forgets, and it always remembers. These are the people to really focus on.

I've found that once you get your PACK down, everything else seems to follow naturally. Once you focus on finding some good, high-quality friends who can grow with you, everything else naturally comes into play.

For example, I've got a childhood friend who I routinely hang out with to this day. He's part of my "pack," but through him, I've met plenty of people in my tribe and in my harem. Through your PACK, you will meet a ton of other like-minded people who will easily fall into your tribe or your harem.

The most important thing is that you do not miscategorize people. If someone is supposed to be in your harem, and you put them in your PACK, eventually you will get fucked.

I typically screen HARD for the people that I let into my life, because if they show any toxic, negative, or disrespectful qualities that I believe would undermine me, I can't afford to allow that into my personal life. It will topple me, period.

I recommend your "pack" have the following attributes:

- Loyalty (the most important)
- Willing to Grow

That's basically it. Everything else is just a bonus, because if someone has those two characteristics, everything else will naturally fall into place.

Again, for example, let's go back to my childhood friend. He had a similar story to me – we were both bullied a lot, and had pretty rough upbringings. We connected over that, and over the years, he's shown his loyalty to me, and that he's willing to grow.

Because of that, as I've grown in my business life and personal life, so has he. Now, when we get together, great things happen. When we hung out in high school, we used to shoot the shit, smoke weed, and listen to music.

Now when we hang out, we talk business ideas, plan vacations, and offer value. The most important thing is that your friends offer you value, otherwise they aren't friends.

Likewise, the best way to MAKE plenty of friends, is to offer plenty of value. Whatever it is that someone wants, if you can give it to them, they will feel indebted to you, and try to give back.

Now, on the topic of getting girls through your social circle, I've found that if you get the GUYS in order, the girls will naturally follow. I prefer to feed girls that I meet through night game, day game, and online dating, INTO my *already-existing* social circle.

That way, I can offer THEM value, but I can also offer my PACK value, by bringing women into their lives. It's a win-win for everyone. Everyone is happy, and everyone wins.

Social circle game can also be a great way to meet new women. For example, some of the sexiest women I know, I've met through my male friends. Why? Because if you have high-quality male friends who own businesses and have exciting lives, they will probably have a lot of girls around them.

In summary, I don't view social circle game as "game" really, but rather just a supportive structure that you can ENHANCE with game. Use night game, day game, and online dating to funnel women into your social circle, and enhance it that way.

Online Dating

Ah, online dating – I've written quite a lot about this. In fact, I'm quite infamous for having banged over 100 hot girls on Tinder in a very short period of time. In fact, I show you exactly how I did it in my "Art of Tinder" eBook, which comes for free when you purchase my 7 Strategies Program (go to getsevenstrategies.com for more info).

Personally, I THRIVE on this type of dating. Why? Because I've mastered it over the years and split-tested literally thousands of different profiles, openers, comebacks, and bios.

In a nutshell, here are the pros of online dating:

- It's fast and efficient
- You can do it anywhere

Here are the cons:

- Most guys can't do it
- It can be frustrating at first

To briefly recap what I've learned, here are a few important notes. The first thing is that, when it comes to online dating, hypergamy is extremely real. In other words, because women have their choice of mates in the palm of their hand (literally), they can screen very hard.

The good news, however, is that you can screen hard too. In a nutshell, you want to demonstrate as much SMV as you possibly can, screen women HARD for their sexual availability and interest, and then get their number or Snapchat as fast as possible.

When creating your profile, you want images that show the following:

- Good Looks (Muscular, Handsome, Grooming, etc.)
- Pre-Selection (Lots of other pretty girls around you)
- Fun/Adventure (You Doing Cool Things)
- High Status (Wealth, Leader of Men, etc.)

If you can successfully communicate these four things, you will be in the top 1% of men on Tinder who sleeps with literally all of the hot girls there.

As I said previously, looks are more important when women are thinking of short-term mates, so if you want to REALLY maximize your potential on Tinder, get my eBook "Body of an Alpha," follow the workout routine for 90 days, and take some pictures of yourself shredded as hell.

When my clients do this, they find that their matches will literally 10x in quantity, and at least 3x in quality. I know it's shallow, but when girls see you've got a sexy, chiseled physique, with broad shoulders and a six pack of abs, they get wet, and they swipe right on you.

In addition to maximizing your appearance on Tinder, I recommend you keep your profile "congruent" as a whole. In other words, think of a "theme" you want for your profile. For me, it's the gym-going, crazy, fun-loving lifestyle entrepreneur. Everything fits within that image.

For you, it may be the "bad boy degenerate" or the "preppy boy" instead. Whatever it is, what's important is that you still show the four things mentioned previously, and are congruent.

As for your bio, have something fun, flirtatious, and maybe a little bit obnoxious. For example, here are a few bios that worked well for me in the past:

- "HMU if you're a bad bitch"
- "Currently accepting girlfriend applications"
- "I'm a musician, become a groupie while you still can"
- "Stop asking because I'm not that kind of girl"

Any one of these will work great as a bio, because they're funny, silly, and slightly break rapport with women. You never want to have a long, drawn-out bio with your entire life's story, because that takes all of the intrigue and mystery away for the girl.

Now that your profile and bio are set in order, you need to swipe properly.

Yes, that's right – you need to swipe properly. None of this "deliberation" bullshit where you decide if each girl is hot enough or you. No, fuck that shit.

What you need to do is LITERALLY swipe right on all of them. This will do two things:

1. Save Time
2. Create Abundance

The goal with Tinder is to be EFFICIENT, and it's incredibly inefficient if you deliberate over each and every girl before swiping right on her. Just swipe right and calibrate later.

This will also give you a lot more matches, and some of the uglier girls will open YOU. I know this might sound shallow, but having 15 girls trying to bang you creates abundance (even if they're ugly).

For the opener, I recommend you use something that screens her HARD. In other words, be flirtatious and sexual right off the bat. Most guys get confused and upset when they use my openers, and they'll tell me something like the following:

> *"Jon, I bought your Tinder guide, and only a few of the girls responded! Is this supposed to happen? I thought they were all going to be on my dick?"*

No. That's not the point. The reason you use a sexual opener is because it IMMEDIATELY does one of two things. If she's interested in you sexually, she responds. Good.

If she's NOT sexually interested, then she won't respond. Good. That's what you want, so you don't waste your time. Getting a lot of girls responding to a compliment or a nice opener is what's called a "false metric." It creates the APPEARANCE of abundance, when actually, none of these girls actually want to fuck you.

By using a sexual opener, you screen hard. The only girls who will respond (AKA the only girls who you'll spend your time on) are sexually interested.

Here are a few of the openers I recommend:

- "You look like a [insert astrological sign here]."
- "Ma'am, it appears that you have a serious case of dick deprivation. The good news is that it's curable, but the bad news is that it requires an invasive procedure."

- "Nice guys or bad boys?"

Once you get the hang of it, you can use your own openers too. The whole point is simple: you want to screen them, so the only ones who respond are the ones who are sexually interested.

Don't waste your time with teases and girls who ignore you. They're not interested, and it's better to focus your energy and efforts on girls who are.

Once she responds to you, keep the conversation going, but try to figure out a way to ask for her number smoothly. The way I like to do this is to pose a question, in which the answer is that she has to give me her number.

For example, here's a typical conversation for me using the previous opener:

> Jon: "Nice guys or bad boys?"
> Girl: "Definitely a little bit of both."
> Jon: "Haha, good choice. And which do you think I am?"
> Girl: "Hmm... I don't know. "
> Jon: "Well, there's only one way to find out."
> Girl: "And what's that?"
> Jon: "You give me your number."

Just remembering this simple conversation technique will 10x your close rate. If you can figure out a way to pose a question that she has to answer by giving you her number, it will make the process _SO MUCH smoother_, and you will encounter very little resistance.

From here, I typically CALL THEM. This does a few things:

1. It shows you're confident
2. It shows that you're real
3. It's faster and cuts through the BS

Most guys are too insecure to call a girl, so when you call her, it shows that you're confident and it makes you stand out from the crowd.

Second, it shows that you're real. When she hears you talk, and hears the confidence sweltering from that deep, baritone voice, she'll feel far more comfortable with meeting you.

Lastly, calling her cuts through the BS of waiting, and texting back and forth. I prefer to set a definitive time and date on the phone, and then text her the day of to remind/ping her.

Another tactic I like to use in online dating is to get her Snapchat instead of her number. Girls have had so many bad experiences with giving out their numbers, so it's almost like there's a universal trauma imprint on every girl when it comes to giving it out.

Snapchat, however? It hasn't been around that long, and most girls enjoy stalking your story. This does a few things. First, you can send her pictures that can't be faked, so she knows you're real. Second, you can build comfort passively by her watching your stories.

Once she gets your Snapchat, it's just a matter of time before you set up a date with her. I prefer to use the old "watch a movie or something" line, and most girls are down for it if you've used the screening process that I taught you.

Social Media

Lastly, there's social media... and although I wouldn't really classify it as a type of "game," I think it's imperative to mention it, because it's changing the landscape of game as we know it.

As much as I hate the smartphone-obsessed culture that we've become, I do think that social media has a lot of benefits for guys who know how to use it properly.

In general, here are the pros of social media game:

- It's GREAT for keeping girls on the hook
- It's easy to do and has residual effects

On the flipside, here are the cons:

- It isn't great for actually MEETING new women, just for keeping them around
- If you aren't living an exciting life, it's hard to do

Overall, I treat social media as a way to keep the girls I'm already dating and fucking interested in me. It's not that great for meeting new girls, but as far as keeping girls "on the hook" goes, nothing else in the world can beat it.

The first thing I need to clarify, however, is that there are two types of people:

1. Producers
2. Consumers

The producers of the world create content. They publish stories, images, and posts. The consumers mindlessly scroll down through their Facebook and Instagram feed all day long.

You want to be a producer. If you can successfully leverage your social media in such a way that it portrays pre-selection, high value, and an exciting lifestyle, you can literally 10x your love life.

That's not even an exaggeration, either. Think of all the girls who you've fallen out of touch with. All the girls you slept with once, or went on a date with once. If they were friends with you on Instagram, and they saw you posting pictures every week of you in the Grand Canyon, on a Yacht in Cannes, and with some girl at Burning Man, do you think they'd still ignore you?

FUCK NO. When women see that you're living an exciting, entertaining, and attractive lifestyle, they want to become a part of it. I know, I know – it's shallow, and it sucks to admit it, but hey, it's just part of the game.

Men judge women on their looks, and they judge us on our lifestyles. I don't make the rules, but I damn sure intend to win the game.

If you want some examples of how to build a "high status" social media profile, you can follow me on Instagram (@RealJonAnthony). I just started it recently, so you'll be able to follow my journey and watch how it grows as I post more and more content.

I recommend you secure all the girls you're banging on Instagram, and then just keep posting interesting stuff. Facebook is for more family-friendly stuff – you with your niece, at your mother's birthday party, and spending time with the family during Christmas.

Instagram, however? It's for the degenerate, high value, braggadocious shit. Don't be afraid to peacock and show off. Social media is the one time you're allowed to do this, so take advantage of it and don't be scared to put yourself out there.

Chapter 12. How to Meet Women

Now that we've discussed where to meet women, and the different types of game, let's get a little bit deeper into the nuts and bolts of how to meet women.

There's a ton of different frameworks out there for meeting women, from the "Mystery Method" to Real Social Dynamics and their methods, but the best, most simplified version out there, is what I've called the "OSSE Framework."

I created it for my video course Alpha Evolution, when I was first asking myself what the simplest and easiest way would be for men to meet women.

The "OSSE Framework" consists of four components:

1. Open
2. Social Hook Point
3. Sexual Hook Point
4. Extraction

Each of these four components has its own unique challenges and characteristics, but once you understand the basic premise of this framework, it's quite easy to use.

OSSE Framework Overview

As an overview, the "open" is simply when you open the girl. It's whatever you first say to her, to grab her attention. Then, there's the "social hook point," which is where she begins to add to the conversation more, and enjoys socializing with you.

Next, is the "sexual hook point" where she becomes sexually invested in you, and is actively flirting BACK. Then, there's the extraction, which is where you go somewhere alone with her, and ideally, end up making love.

Now, keep in mind that this is primarily applicable to NIGHT GAME and DAY GAME. It works the best for night game, however – because this is your "bread and butter" as a pickup artist.

Step 1. Open

Your open is really quite simple. It's the first words that come out of your mouth, and contrary to popular belief, they actually aren't that important.

What matters the most when you first open a girl, isn't WHAT you say, but _how you say it._ As I've made abundantly clear, women are very attuned to the sub-communication that takes place during a conversation, so that's what they'll be picking up on.

If you're feeling nervous, they will feel it. If you're feeling at ease, they will feel it. If you're feeling desire, they will feel it. I'm not trying to freak you out here, but women are almost psychic in their ability to pick up social cues off of men.

So, what really matters the most, is not to worry about it. Just treat it as an experiment, in which you learn something new about socializing every time you conduct it.

Overall, there are six different types of openers:

1. Opinion
2. Compliment
3. Functional
4. Direct
5. Introductory
6. Observational

Each opener has its own unique applications, strengths, and weaknesses. Again, which opener you use isn't that important – what matters the most is the way you say it. Focus on being present, direct, maintaining steady eye contact, and having a smile on your face.

The opinion opener is just what it sounds like. It's where you ask her opinion on something. The classic examples of this would be something like:

- "Who cheats more – guys or girls?"
- "Is it cheating if your boyfriend has pictures of his ex on his phone?"

They're short, sweet, and are meant to elicit an emotional response from her, and get her hooked into the conversation. They work great, but the downside is they don't convey interest.

The compliment opener, however, does convey interest. It's just what it sounds like – you give her a compliment. Ideally, you want it to be a genuine compliment, and one that you put a little bit of effort into. Again, it's how you say it that really matters.

For example, walking up to a girl and telling her: "I like your dress, it matches your eyes," is a much better compliment than just saying: "You're beautiful." If you can compliment the way a girl's X matches her Y, that's great, because most guys don't pick up on this.

Overall, I'm not the biggest fan of compliment openers. They automatically put the power into her playing field. Instead, I prefer to give girls compliments once I know them better, and once I feel like they've been sufficiently nice to "earn it."

As a side note, this ties into the core of being alpha vs. beta. Most guys, when they first get into dating and self-help, ask a very common question:

"Jon, you say that I shouldn't compliment a girl, but then you say it all the time? Why is this? I don't understand, what gives? Do I compliment her or not?"

The truth is that, if a compliment is coming from the _right place_, it's a good thing. If you feel inspired to compliment a girl, and you just do it, then she will generally receive it very well.

If however, you are complimenting her, because you're trying to get in her pants, she will likely not receive the compliment very well at all. This is what Nice Guys™ do, and it doesn't work.

I have no problem complimenting a girl. In fact, I often SHOWER girls in compliments when I'm sleeping with them. When I'm banging a girl, there's basically no filter at all – anything I'm thinking, I just automatically say it.

"Oh my God, wow, your ass is literally perfect," I'll say, as I'm smacking it and pulling her hair. This type of compliment gives her a rush of validation and excitement, because it's GENUINE.

In addition to this, since she's already decided to sleep with me, she knows I'm not saying it to get in her pants, but because I actually mean it.

Anyways, back to the openers. The next one is a functional opener. This can work great if you're not hitting on a girl, but just want to strike up a conversation and see where it leads, but overall, I'm still not a big fan of it.

The functional opener is an opener used for a specific function. For example:

- "Hey, do you know the Wi-Fi code here?"
- "Hey, do you know where the nearest coffee shop is?"
- "Do you like these jeans? I can't figure out if I'd look good in them."

I will occasionally use functional openers when I'm out, if I see a beautiful woman I want to talk to who's on the move. I'll walk up, walk *in front of her*, and ask her where the best club is.

That's about it, though. Overall, I don't really use functional openers. I prefer direct openers, because they're efficient and straight-forward, which is congruent to who I am.

Direct openers are just what they sound like – fucking direct. One of my favorite direct openers to use, whether I'm at the gym, traveling, or out at the mall, is the following:

> *"Hey, just one sec – I have to go meet some friends in a minute, but I thought you looked cute and wanted to talk to you real quick. What's your name?"*

This opener screens girls very hard for interest. If they aren't interested, they'll quickly come up with an excuse, such as: "I have a boyfriend," or "I have to go."

If they're even slightly interested however, they'll stick around and talk to you. I use this opener to quickly chat a girl up, get to know her, and grab her number for a meetup later.

I also love this opener because it does a few things. The first is that it clarifies you won't take up her time all day, because you have to "go meet some friends in a minute."

One of a girl's greatest fears when she's getting hit on, is that the guy won't leave. If you tell her that you're already leaving in a few minutes however, it takes all the pressure off.

The second thing it does, is it communicates that you have FRIENDS – AKA you're not a random person who could potentially be a lone serial killer. I know this may sound stupid, but trust me, this is how girls think.

The third thing I like about it, is it gives her a compliment, but not an overbearing one. Just calling her "cute" and not "beautiful" or "gorgeous" is enough to convey interest, but not so much that you come off as a nice guy or supplicating beta male.

Next is the introductory opener. This isn't very useful, because you can't use it that often, but when you can use it, there's almost a 100% chance of it being successful.

This is a sort of sly opener you use to meet a girl's friends, so it isn't _technically_ an opener per se, but you are using it to open her friends.

Just tell the girl you're already talking to: "Hey, can I meet your friends real quick?" and get her to introduce you to them. That's it. That's the introductory opener.

Lastly is the observational opener. This is another one of my favorites, because you can have a lot of fun with it. It can also get girls qualifying right off the bat, which is quite nice.

For the observational opener, you simply say something about their appearance or demeanor. For example, if she looks like a hippie, you might say something like: "You look like the type of girl who only shops at Whole Foods."

If she seems like a "bad bitch," you might say something like: "I feel like you could fuck me up, you look like a really dangerous girl." It's pretty simple once you get the hang of it, and the applications are endless.

As I said before, with the observational opener, it's a great "hook" to get her qualifying. She might start jumping through your hoops, and proving how she's exactly what you said she is, OR she might desperately try to prove that she's NOT what you said.

Either way, if you can get her qualifying herself to you, that's good.

Overall, memorizing these different types of openers will help you greatly in approaching women. Most of approach anxiety is just not knowing what to say. Well, now you know.

Step 2. Social Hook Point

After your opener, she may respond favorably or unfavorably. Either way, I want you to get one thing through your head, _LOUD AND CLEAR:_

You, as the man, have the burden of conversation. It is 100% on you to keep the conversation going. It is not her job to seduce herself. It is your job to do this.

Too many guys use an opener on a girl, and then just magically expect her to start sucking his dick on the spot. This isn't how it's going to work.

Most of the time, you're going to use your opener. Then, she's going to say something back. Then, there's going to be a little bit of silence, and you'll have to keep the conversation going.

This is 99% of what the social hook point comes down to. You simply want to focus on _keeping the conversation going_, and keeping it light-hearted and fun. It doesn't matter what you say, but just that you keep talking, and keep the vibe lighthearted and fun.

Women are far more attuned to sub-communications than men are, so you can literally get away with saying anything, if you know how. In fact, in my video "How to Talk to Girls (Never Run Out of Things to Say Again)," I give you an exercise you can use to train your ability to talk to women for hours on end, without ever running out of anything to say.

Eventually, if you can do this for a few minutes, and if you guys have enough natural chemistry, you will reach the "social hook point." This is the point where she's not just in the conversation as a passive observer, but rather as an active participant.

Some girls will reach this point immediately, if you're physically attractive and confident enough as a man. Other girls will be more standoffish, and slower to open up.

The main thing to keep in mind, is that when you first open her, you will be doing about 80% of the conversation. Eventually, as she becomes more comfortable, she will participate more.

She will go from contributing 20% of the conversation, to eventually, contributing 80% or more of the conversation. When you can get a girl talking a lot, this is a good thing – it means she's in her feminine element, and is freely expressing her thoughts and emotions.

Again, the main thing about the social hook point, is to fight through the awkwardness and keep the conversation going.

It doesn't matter what you talk about, just that you do it in a fun and positive way. That being said, I recommend you screen her and get the basics:

- If she's in college (this is a sly way to figure out her age)
- What she does for work
- What she does for fun

Just focusing on these three things is enough for most men. Another tip is to focus on building COMMONALITIES, because this will build comfort with a girl.

It doesn't matter how stupid the commonality seems. It could be that you both love dogs, or that you both enjoy lifting weights. Just try to build commonalities.

If you're doing day game, once you reach the social hook point, you have two options:

1. End the conversation and ask for her number

2. Go on an instant date (right then and there)

Personally, I prefer to do #1 because I'm a busy guy, but if you feel that the chemistry is solid, and she's a sexy girl who's just your type, you can try going on an instant date.

Just tell her: "Hey, what are you doing right now? Let's go to Starbucks – it's right over here."

Grab her by the hand and _lead her._ Women want to be led by a strong man. Again, the burden of seduction is on you – so act like it.

To go on an instant date, simply find a venue that's nearby. It could be a Starbucks, a smoothie shop, or whatever. Just tell her it's "right here" and lead her towards it.

Once you're on the instant date, aim to reach the sexual hook point, which is discussed more in depth in the next chapter.

If you're doing night game, it's the same thing. Once you reach the social hook point, your goal is to either end the conversation and get her number, or reach the sexual hook point.

Step 3. Sexual Hook Point

In many ways, the sexual hook point is very similar to the social hook point. In both of these, the burden is on you to make it happen. In both of these as well, she will start off doing 20% of the work, and will eventually reach 50% or even 80%.

Where the social hook point was concerned with "socializing," the sexual hook point is concerned with "sexualizing."

Where the social hook point was concerned with getting her talking, the sexual hook point is concerned with getting her flirting.

Once you've reached the social hook point, and she's doing an equal amount of the conversation, you want to start sexualizing things a bit.

As a side note, an experienced pickup artist can start sexualizing the conversation _right off the bat_, and can even skip the social hook point altogether.

Regardless, most newbies cannot do this, so I decided to split the "OSSE Framework" into four distinct categories. Again, for the sexual hook point, the burden is on you.

Start by flirting with her a little bit; tease her, bring the conversation towards dating/sex, and start upping the kino.

Kino is simply nerd PUA talk for touching her in a slightly sexual way, such as putting your hands on her hips, on her lower back, and/or wrapping your arm around her shoulder.

I personally try to start touching a girl very quickly after meeting her. Again, it isn't always super sexual right off the bat, but all that's needed to build closeness and comfort is light touching.

Referring to the note I made previously, you always want to escalate on a high note. So, for example, touching her leg or her arm as you both laugh at a joke is a good example.

Another example might be telling her: "I fucking hate you," and pushing her away, and when she comes running back, tell her: "I fucking love you," and give her a big old hug.

This type of "push-pull" game should be your bread and butter to spike her emotions. Again, girls love it when you give them the full range of emotions. I will routinely tell girls that I fucking hate them (with a smile of course) and then that I fucking love them right afterward.

The goal of "pushing" her is to show her that you're not afraid to lose her. Most guys only "pull, pull, pull," and don't ever push, but simply adding a little bit of "push" to your game can literally have the power to 10x your results.

Here are some common pushes that newbies can try:

- "Oh, you're from [XYZ]? I don't think we'll get along."
- "Oh God, please tell me you're joking."
- "Don't start any fights now, okay?"

As you get more experienced, your pushes will be a lot harder, because you'll be calibrated and experienced enough to pull it off. I've literally pushed girls away from me, and yelled at them, calling them a "fucking whore" and a "dirty little slut," but because I've got them emotionally and sexually invested in me, hook, line, and sinker, they crack up and start laughing.

Again, if you're a newbie, I do NOT recommend you try these things. While it's very powerful when you can do it, if you miscalibrate and use it in the wrong way, it will quite literally blow the fuck up in your face.

The primary purpose of the sexual hook point is simply to start sexualizing the conversation, getting her comfortable with touching you, and spiking her emotions more.

I try to sexualize my conversations as soon as possible, because the longer you wait to do it, the more awkward it will feel when you do.

On the other hand, if you start holding hands, touching her waist, and getting close to her very quickly, when you eventually get alone with her and make a move, it will feel more natural.

What I recommend most guys do for the sexual hook point, is start by testing the waters. Throw out a few sexual signs, and if

she doesn't give you "Indicators of Disinterest" (discussed in the next section), or if she reciprocates, then continue with more.

Here are a few ways to "test the water":

- Look deeply into her eyes
- Lightly touch her waist/arm/shoulder as you're talking to her
- Get very physically close to her
- Try holding her hips as you talk to her
- Try kissing her eventually (after light touching)

If she doesn't give you any resistance, then try kissing her. I don't necessarily recommend doing this if you're doing day game, just because she might be too self-conscious.

If it's night game, however, go for it. Just remember not to escalate TOO MUCH if you don't think you can pull her that night. The reason why is because she might feel awkward the next day, because she'll feel like you "expect it."

All in all, the sexual hook point is the biggest sticking point for most men, behind the initial approach. This being said, it isn't actually that hard once you break it down to a science.

Start by lightly touching her arm. Get closer to her as you talk to her. Try holding her hips. Does she back away? If so, back up (to show her you acknowledge her resistance) and try again later when she seems more receptive.

Much of this is an art, rather than a science. As much as we try to analyze game and seduction scientifically, much of it is an art, and many of its principles are paradoxical.

Step 4. Extraction

Lastly, is the extraction. This is the phase where you go somewhere alone with her, so that you can get her into bed and seal the deal.

This is, of course, the hardest part of game. Many women will be resistant to sleeping with you, for different reasons, but what's important is that you realize you can overcome them.

Typically, when women don't want to sleep with you, it's for one of two reasons:

1. Not enough comfort
2. Not enough value

If you're unsure, I suggest you err on the side of "not enough value," and begin using some of the tactics I mentioned previously to spike her emotions and demonstrate higher value.

When you try to "extract" a girl, you want to take it step-by-step, and always have plausible deniability. For example, the first thing I'll do with a girl (when I'm at a night club) is I'll ask her if she wants to go get some fresh air outside.

Then, when we're outside, I'll continue the conversation. Eventually, I'll ask if she wants to go get food. Then, after we finish getting food, I'll ask if she wants to go back to my place.

The critical thing to keep in mind here, is you never want to jump ahead too much. Women are emotional creatures (if you haven't figured that out already) and will grow more comfortable and attracted to you, as they experience you in different situations.

You often need to ease a girl into having sex with you, and the best way to do this is to take her to a myriad of locations. Again, it's called "baby stepping" for a reason.

When you invite her back to your place, ALWAYS have an excuse to be alone with her. Girls aren't stupid – they know what you're trying to do.

But telling her that you want to "watch a movie" or "have another drink" is a much smoother line than just flat out asking her if she wants to fuck.

It doesn't really matter what you tell her – I've had a girl tell me we should go back to her place, to get some "water." Some fucking water!

Do you think she's stupid? Of course not. She just wants an excuse, because it sounds weird and way too obvious to ask: "Hey… so, uhh… do you wanna FUCK?"

Girls are virtually psychic in their ability to read you, so don't for a second think that they don't understand how this game is played. They know that you don't actually want to "watch a movie," and that you're just using it as an excuse to get closer to them.

…and they appreciate it, too. They appreciate when a man can seamlessly seduce them, in a way that makes her feel comfortable, validated, and sexy as a woman.

If you're serious about game, I recommend you maximize your logistics as much as is humanly possible. A newbie with great logistics will get 10x more lays than an expert with bad ones.

Think about it – if you live _right next to the club_, imagine how easy it is to pull girls. It's literally a 3-minute walk to your house, compared to every other guy, who's a 20-minute uber away.

When you live a block away from the night club, it doesn't feel like a "big deal" to a girl. "Oh, it's just a block away," she'll say – and she'll eagerly come with you.

Logistics are king when it comes to extraction. That's why I always plan first dates in such a way that they're NEAR my apartment (but more on this in Part 5).

Ideally, you want to host a lot of parties at your house, because that's the king of logistics. Ask any guy who has a lot of parties at his place, and he'll tell you. He probably gets laid... a lot.

Why? Again, it's simple. Girls want to feel like sex "just happens" when in reality, guys are planning it all the entire time. She wants to feel like it just magically happened, as if the fates ordained it. This is her feminine energy at play, and you must accept it.

Let me tell you a story to illustrate this point.

I remember one time when I was in a fraternity, I met this sexy little blonde chick on the dance floor. We started dancing, talking, and kissing.

"Do you want to go upstairs?" I asked. "Yeah!" she said. We literally walked up a few stairs, and I found an open bedroom, and banged her.

Do you see how simple that is? When you literally live right next to the dance floor, it's so fucking easy to pull chicks. Imagine if I told her: "Hey, do you want to take a 30-minute uber back to my place and watch a movie?" Her response would have been much different.

I recommend you leverage your social circle and try having regular parties at your house each week. It doesn't matter if very few people come at first – just stay consistent, have a lot of alcohol, and keep everyone happy.

Eventually, your place will be poppin' each week, and when girls find out you're not only the host of the party, but that your bedroom is literally a few feet away? It's fucking on.

Chapter 13. How to Know if She's Interested

As you escalate on women, you want to make sure that they're interested in you. Many newbies are uncalibrated, and can't tell if a girl is into them or not.

Unfortunately, in today's #MeToo culture, guys have to focus on being more calibrated than ever. Take Aziz Ansari, for example, who basically just had a "bad date," but was then branded as a rapist and a sex offender by the bloodthirsty media.

This happened because he wasn't calibrated. He couldn't pick up on the finely tuned signs that women give off, to let you know they're not interested (or that they are).

Again, don't be afraid – most guys will never be falsely convicted of rape or sexual harassment. That being said though, it's important to know that there are some crazy chicks out there, and you should make sure that she's 100% down before you continue.

Indicators of Interest

Indicators of Interest, or IOI's for short, are simply signs she gives you that mean she's interested in you. These can be as subtle as giving you deep eye contact, and as obvious as literally pulling down your pants and sucking your dick.

There's a 7 IOI's that I recommend most guys look for:

1. Deep Eye Contact
2. She Touches You
3. She Plays With Her Hair
4. She Giggles Incessantly
5. She Shit Tests You
6. She Calls You A Player

7. She Qualifies Herself to You

The more IOI's that a girl gives you, the more likely she's interested in you. Some other additional IOI's would be things like:

- She always finds excuses to be alone with you
- She asks if you want to dance
- She keeps hovering around you (this means she wants you to approach her)
- When you look at her, she quickly looks away
- She leans her head on your shoulder
- She moans or smiles when you touch her
- When you kiss her, she kisses you back

Some girls are subtler with their IOI's than others, so you have to be aware of this. I've had girls who I NEVER knew were into me, but who I later found out wanted to sleep with me.

Even if you only catch a girl giving you a single IOI, chances are she's interested in you. The reason why is that, again, girls are more socially intelligent than guys are – so you're probably only picking up on HALF or even less of the IOI's she's giving off.

As you're escalating, you should definitely look for IOI's to signal her approval. That being said, what's actually more important (and accurate) is looking for IOD's which might signal her disapproval.

Indicators of Disinterest

Indicators of Disinterest, or IOD's for short, are signs a girl gives off to let you know that she's NOT interested in you. In my opinion, these are far more important to pick up on.

Why? Because if you escalate on a girl, and she's continually giving you IOD's, but you don't notice them, you could be slapped in the face, or even worse.

It's important to keep an eye out for IOD's, but to complicate things even FURTHER, you shouldn't confuse IOD's with "token disinterest." More on this later, though.

Some common IOD's to look out for are:

- Tense body language
- Continues to look away from you
- Facial expressions of disgust, contempt, fear, etc.
- Very brief/curt answers to your questions

If you're escalating on a girl physically, and she begins to give you these Indicators of Disinterest, consider backing away, offering a statement of empathy, and then cooling it off.

Funny enough, most guys get upset when a girl gives them an IOD, but I actually view it as an excellent opportunity to prove to her that I'm a socially savvy man.

Let me give you an example. I've told this story a million times before (if you're a reader of my blog), but it's worth telling again, because it illustrates this point perfectly.

I'm going to give you the straight story first, and THEN the analysis on what happened, and more specifically, WHY it happened.

A few years ago, I was flirting with this beautiful blonde bombshell – let's call her Rachel. I was in the zone, and she was absolutely eating out of the palm of my hand.

I picked her up, and told her friends that she has a nice ass. I then ordered her friends to smack it. They did. Then, I put Rachel down, motorboated her tits, and took a giant step back. She lunged at me to hug me, and we immediately started making out.

Okay. Does that sound interesting to you? How is it that I could literally pick a girl up, and ORDER her friends to smack her butt, and they would comply?

How is it that I could motorboat her tits, and then literally step AWAY from her, and have her so addicted to me, that she LUNGED at me to start hugging me and kissing me?

Most guys if they tried this shit would get a fucking sexual assault charge. But how did I do this? Well, I'm going to explain – kids, don't try this at home.

Rachel was clearly into me. I thought she was absolutely stunning, and could literally feel the feminine energy radiating off of her. We had incredible chemistry.

As we started flirting and making out more, I looked out of the corner of my eye, and saw that her friends were watching me. They were impressed at how charming I was.

I immediately recognized this as an opportunity to merge the sets. So, I picked Rachel up, who at this point could not stop laughing, and I was struck by how nice her ass looked.

I pointed it out to her friends, and said to them: "Doesn't your friend have a nice ass? Like oh my God, WOW! God damn!"

What's important is that I said it with genuine DESIRE and GOOD EMOTIONS – it just came out naturally, because I really did think that Rachel looked good in the tight booty shorts she was wearing.

I also knew from previous game experience, that girls will ALWAYS compliment their friends – it's the female code of conduct. They will call each other beautiful, sexy, and stunning all day long, because as I said before, feminine energy is supportive.

Of course, just as I predicted, they cracked up and started laughing. "Yes! She's so gorgeous, isn't she!" they all chimed in.

Again, what's important is that I was LEADING. I didn't MEEKLY ask if she had a nice ass, and I wasn't asking for their PERMISSION. I was simply BEING a MAN.

I decided to take a risk and ask them to smack it. I knew from previous game experience (do you see how important this is?) that their emotions were sufficiently spiked for me to do this, and there was a high likelihood that they would follow along.

...and again, just as I predicted, they did. They smacked her ass. This, of course, spiked Rachel's emotions even more. She was getting the royal treatment. A high-value man was literally spiking her emotions, and encouraging her friends to do the same.

So, I put her down, and again, she could not stop laughing. I saw how beautiful her boobs looked in the low-cut top she was wearing, and decided to motorboat them.

Here's the magic key, though – as I did this, I noticed she slightly tensed up, and backed away a little bit. She was giving me an Indicator of Disinterest.

So, what did I do? I backed away, to let her know that I UNDERSTAND she felt uncomfortable for a moment. This took the pressure off of her.

I didn't try to escalate further, I didn't chase her, and I didn't apologize. I saw that she was slightly uncomfortable, and to show her that I recognized this, I took a giant step back, as if to say: "I'm sorry, here, I'll give you some space."

She IMMEDIATELY recognized this, and understood that I wasn't going to pressure her into doing anything she didn't want to. This is why she lunged at me to give me a giant hug. She saw that I respected her boundaries, and was in tune with her feelings.

Now, do you see how much information was conveyed with just a simple IOD? What's important isn't so much the Indicator of Disinterest itself, but how you react.

Again, as I said – view IOD's as an opportunity to show her that you're socially savvy, and can tell when a girl isn't quite interested (just yet). You will respect her boundaries.

The best thing to do when a girl gives you an IOD, is to just give her some space, and try again later if she seems more receptive. As you escalate on girls, keep an eye out for IOD's.

Don't take it personally if they give you an IOD. It simply means she isn't warmed up enough just yet. Give it time, respect her boundaries, and she will come to love you.

Chapter 14. Doing The Numbers

I wanted to make a section specifically regarding rejection and "doing the numbers," because it's one of the biggest things that men don't understand about women.

Most men don't understand that getting girls is a NUMBER'S GAME. Yes, of course, you want to focus on getting quality, but in order to even get there, you must first get quantity.

A common question I get asked is something like this:

> *"Jon, how do I get this one girl that I'm in love with from school? She's so beautiful and I have tried to ask her out, but just can't get the courage to do it. What should I do?"*

Asking a question like this completely misses the point. Becoming more attractive and successful with women is a skillset, and like any other skillset, it must be learned.

Imagine if a man asked the following question:

> *"Jon, how do I beat Mike Tyson in a boxing match? I just need to beat him so much, and I've tried to figure it out, but I just can't understand. What do you think I should do?"*

What would you say to such a man? You'd tell him to get his ass in the boxing ring and start fucking PRACTICING. There's no way in HELL you're going to beat Mike Tyson without a ton of practice, and you'll probably have to face a few dozen professional boxers before you even get a chance to get in the ring with Mike.

Now... do you see how this applies to women? Most guys obsess over getting that "one special girl," and while it is romantic in a sense, you need to expand your horizons.

Don't focus on getting one girl. Focus on getting good with women as a SKILLSET, so that then you can get any girl you want.

You're not going to beat Mike Tyson without ever having a boxing match in your entire life, are you? So how do you think you'll be able to get your dream girl without first approaching, attracting, and seducing dozens of other girls first?

Doing the numbers is an integral part of learning game, and it's something every man must come to terms with. At times, you will feel rejected and disgruntled. That's okay.

It takes time and a lot of repetition before you start to really get good with this stuff. The good news, however, is that you can get good FAST if you apply the knowledge in this book.

Part 5: Dating Girls

"Internet dating is the fastest, most efficient way to gather a pool of qualified candidates. It could take you a lifetime to do the investigation that the computer comes up with in seconds."

-Judsen Culbreth

"Dating is really all about sex. In the conventional context, this means that the man invites the woman to go through a social encounter, the ultimate purpose of which is sexual engagement."

-Alexander McCall Smith

"Dating is a give and take. If you only see it as "taking," you are not getting it."

-Henry Cloud

Executive Summary

This part is relatively short, simply because dating women is relatively simple. Generally speaking, dating serves two purposes: to sleep with women you have not slept with yet, and to build a better connection with women you've already slept with.

This is why I have divided dates up into two categories: the "first date" and the "fun date." Your first date should be focused on screening her, getting to know her, and sleeping with her.

Beyond this, if you choose to date her for a longer period of time, your "fun dates" should be focused on having fun, strengthening your bond, and solidifying your position in her mind as an alpha male.

Ideally, your "first date" should be hooking up at your place, although with many girls this will not be the case. You want to start off as a "lover" so that you can easily transition into the "provider" if you so wish. Most guys have this completely inverted.

The goal of the very first date, or the very first time you meet her, is simply to get to know her better, and ideally, sleep with her by the end of the night. If you know she's a conservative woman, this may change, and you may want to play the "long game" of courting her, but for most situations, you want to sleep with her as soon as possible.

The first date should be held in a location that is close to your house, so that you can easily transition to hanging out there, rather than out in public. This will make sex happen more naturally, and it will feel like "it just happened" on her end, when in reality, you're just meticulously planning everything out.

Beyond this, dating a woman really serves only one purpose: to strengthen your bond. You do this by leveraging two critical aspects of female nature: you want her to feel a variety of emotions, while you're simultaneously leading her through them. Ideally, your "fun dates" should make her feel excitement, awe, fear, jealousy, and love, all the while you're guiding her through them, so that she feels protected and safe.

Chapter 15. Acing The First Date

The purpose of the first date will depend on how and when you met her. We must also define "date" because, in today's sexual marketplace, this is a vague term.

A date, in the sense that I'm using it, is when you take a girl out to a public location, to have fun and get to know her better. The key here is it's something you go OUT to do.

This is NOT the same as when you invite a girl over from Tinder, and sleep with her the very first night that you meet her. It's also not the same as when you meet a girl out clubbing, and sleep with her that very night. These things aren't dates, but rather hookups.

Typically, I only take the following types of girls on a "first date":

- Girls I met from Tinder who don't want to fuck me right away
- Girls I met from my social circle who don't want to fuck me right away
- Numbers I got from gaming, of girls who don't want to fuck me right away

Do you see the point here? If a girl is immediately interested in sleeping with you, then for the love of God, sleep with her! Then, if you like her, and have chemistry, you can take her on exciting dates afterward to solidify your already existing bond.

For me, the biggest thing is to sleep with her ASAP. This may sound manipulative, but again, think back to our earlier chapters on the "Lover vs. Provider" dichotomy.

When you get in the habit of taking her out on dates without ever sleeping with her, she begins to slot you into the "provider" category, and as every man knows, it's EXTREMELY difficult to jump from the provider category into the lover category.

If, however, you sleep with her very quickly, she will naturally categorize you as a "lover." Then, once you become her lover, it's much easier to start taking her out on fun dates.

That being said, some girls will not want to sleep with you right away. This is fine. That's their choice, and you need to accept this as a man. If she doesn't sleep with you after a few dates, then, to be honest, she just isn't that into you. Accept it, and move on.

Some girls will make you wait for 2-3 dates until they sleep with you. I typically don't wait this long to sleep with a girl, unless she is _extremely worth it._

If a girl is the full package – sweet, sexy, feminine, and my "dream girl" – then I am perfectly fine taking her on a few dates before we sleep together. Even still, this is not ideal. You want to get slotted as the "lover" as soon as possible, and THEN you can take her out on dates.

For the girls who don't want to sleep with me right away, but who show promise, I will typically take them out on a simple first date, such as grabbing coffee.

The goal of the first date is not to woo her and give her an incredible time. The purpose of the first date is to meet her, develop comfort and commonalities, and screen her.

Chapter 16. Location, Location, Location

One of the reasons why I choose to do the first date at Starbucks, is because it's inexpensive, and doesn't require a lot of time or commitment on my end. I don't want to shell out a bunch of dough, or spend a lot of time, on a girl I barely even know.

The whole purpose of the first date, as I said, is to get to know her better, and then if we have chemistry, to close the deal. This is why I always choose a Starbucks that's convenient.

Typically, my first dates go like this:

1. We meet and greet
2. I chat her up, maybe flirt a bit
3. If we have chemistry, I ask if she wants to watch a movie at my place
4. If she says yes, great. If she says no, tell her "that's fine" and keep talking

For the women reading this, you might view my advice as "manipulative," but understand that many men have been badly burned by girls. They will take women out on expensive dates and dinners, and she will manipulate them into spending hundreds or even THOUSANDS of dollars.

Now, I don't have anything against spending money on a girl – in fact, I'll frequently take the girls I'm sleeping with on awesome vacations. I'll take them traveling with me, I'll buy them dinners, and I'll take them on romantic dates.

The reason why I'm willing to do this, however, is because I know they're not in it for that. If you only ever LEAD with buying her nice stuff, you'll never know if she actually likes you as a person, or if she's just in it for the gifts and rewards.

When a girl is willing to sleep with you, without receiving any sort of "date" in return, it shows that she's incredibly attracted to *who you are as a person.* This is why I rarely take girls on first dates, unless we met on Tinder and they want to meet in public at first.

On the rare occasion that I do take a girl on a first date, however, I'll make it quick and simple, as I said. The goal is to build rapport in person, so that she's comfortable going back to my place, and having a great night with me.

Try to choose a Starbucks that's close to you, so it's easy to get back. Another thing I often do, is I time the date, so it's only 30 minutes before the Starbucks closes. That way, we don't get stuck talking for hours and hours.

We talk for 30 minutes, she gets to know me, and then it's closing time. I hit her with a very simple, but proven line: "Hey, do you want to step outside and keep talking? They're closing soon." If she's interested in you, she will say yes.

Again, remember back to the concept of baby stepping. I'll typically stay outside and chat with her for a few minutes, and then tell her: "Hey listen, I'm like 5 minutes away from here. Do you wanna go watch a movie or meet my puppy or something?

Remember, guys – girls aren't stupid. She knows that if she goes somewhere with you, as a man, you will probably try to make a move on her. They appreciate it when you can offer a "convenient excuse" to get some alone time with her.

Of course, she can still say no – that's her right as a woman. But just the fact that she's willing to be alone with you means she's somewhat sexually interested, even if she's not fully ready.

Now, let's address a common question that I often get:

"Jon, how do I approach the first date with a girl I met out at the club? We were dancing, laughing, flirting, having fun, and making out. What should I do?"

The general rule is to pick up the conversation where it started off. If you were already flirting and having fun, then just keep that vibe going.

Of course, you may have to backtrack slightly, because remember – her emotions were spiked the night you met her, but you may have to spike them again during the first date.

As a whole, however, treat the "first date" as a continuation of your previous interaction.

Chapter 17. Second Date and Beyond

Now, as I said, if you're interested in a girl, you want to sleep with her as soon as possible. This will make her view you as a "confident, charming man" who goes after what he wants in life.

On the rare occasion, however, that you're dating a STUNNER who's worth it to wait on, you can continue taking her out on dates until she's ready to sleep with you.

Either way, in my book, after the "first date" there's really only one other type of date... and that's the "fun date." The purpose of the fun date is different than the first date.

The purpose of the fun date is to spike her emotions, have fun, and strengthen your bond.

The reason why I don't typically do a "fun date" as a "first date" is because I don't want to waste a whole lot of time on a girl if I barely even know her yet.

If she passes my "screening" processes during the first date, and if she fits my standards and criteria, then I'll consider taking her on a "fun date" sometime.

Your "fun dates" can be whatever you want, but generally speaking, there are two major things you want to really ace:

1. She's Feeling Emotions
2. You're Leader Her Through Them

If you can do these two things for a girl on a Fun Date™, there's an almost 100% chance she will begin to fall in love with you, and if she hasn't already, to sleep with you.

The reason why is actually quite simple. Again, remember what women want – they want to feel. It doesn't even really matter WHAT they feel, just that you make them feel something.

If you combine this with you "leading her through them" however, she will literally remember this date you took her on for the rest of her life.

The reason why these two things, when used in conjunction, are so powerful, is because they combine her feeling emotions, with you LEADING her through them.

This naturally satisfies both of her feminine desires: to FEEL, and to be LED by an alpha male.

Why do you think guys who have motorcycles get laid so much? Is it because motorcycles give off a bad boy image? Of course, that's part of it.

But the BIGGEST part of it, is that when a woman is riding a motorcycle with a guy, she's FEELING an intense array of emotions. From the fear of taking a sharp turn, to the exhilaration of going over the speed limit, her whole body is electrified with emotions.

Combine this with the fact that you're in control, you're driving the motorcycle, and she's trusting you to drive her around safely, and it's no wonder she's wet as a well right after (it also doesn't hurt that the whole motorcycle is vibrating her groin the entire time).

One thing I like to do with girls is take them out into scenic places in nature. Ideally, it's a place I've already been – this makes me the leader, and the commander of the situation. She follows my lead, because I've been there, and she trusts me to make the right decisions along the way.

For example, there's a famous mountain near where I live, and when you drive to the top of it during the nighttime, you can see the night sky in all of its splendor.

So, I'll take girls up in my car, and the entire time, I'll talk about how beautiful it is. Again, what am I doing? I'm giving them a massive hit of emotions (in this case, anticipation).

Then, when we get there, I'll open her door, grab her hand, and walk her outside so she can look up at the night sky. "It's beautiful," she'll say. Again, she's feeling.

She's feeling wonder. She's feeling awe. And she's feeling it while I'm holding her from behind. I'm guiding her through the entire experience, and she loves it.

Thoughts race through her mind. "I wonder if he does this for all his girls... he can't! He mustn't! Does he? I must be so special for him to do this with me... Wow, I'm so in love with him."

Mastering the art of the "Fun Date" is literally the key to making women fall in love with you.

Again, I don't recommend you do this with girls you barely know. On occasion, if you know a "good girl" who probably won't sleep with you unless she has an emotional connection with you, then you can do this to woo her.

For the most part, however, I save the really fun dates for the girls I'm already sleeping with, so that I know they already like me for who I am, and not what I do for them.

Part 6: Plate Spinning

"When you have three girls that you can call at any point to come over to your house, you don't give a fuck if one rejects you at a bar."

-Derek Cajun

"Surrounding myself with beautiful women keeps me young."

-Hugh Hefner

Executive Summary

Plate-spinning is the idea that you want to date multiple girls at once. I'm not advocating for cheating, and if you're in a long-term, exclusive relationship, you should honor that commitment. But most men find that casually dating a handful of women is an enjoyable and rewarding experience, that allows them to date higher quality women.

The "Iron Rule of Harems" is to keep it vague. When you're dating a lot of different women, you want to leverage their imagination for you, and have it do the work. Simply demonstrate high value, alpha male characteristics (discussed in Part 2 of this book) and if she ever asks about your sex life, be vague. Call your lovers your "friends." She will know what this means.

Fundamentally, building a harem comes down to four simple steps: the pull, retention, repetition, and filtration. When used in conjunction, this four-step process is meant to not only build your harem, but slowly upgrade the quality of your harem.

The first step of building a harem, is pulling. This simply means sleeping with women. This is discussed in Part 5, so if you have not read that section, then please do so.

Once you pull women, you want to focus on your "retention" which is getting them to keep coming back. Retention comes down to three things: having chemistry, giving her good sex, and providing her with value. If you can do these three things, your retention rate will be high.

Third, is repetition. Just pull more girls, work on retaining them, and eventually, you'll start collecting a handful of women who want to keep coming around. This is the start of your harem – cherish it, and blow fire onto the embers, to grow it.

Lastly, comes the process of filtration. This is where you slowly start to filter the lower quality girls out of your harem, in favor of higher quality girls.

You may choose to sleep with a girl who's attractive, but has a toxic personality, at the beginning of your harem-building process, but once you have 5-6 women circling you, it's time to start letting these types of women go.

When all is said and done, if you follow this process, you will be able to successfully sleep with, date, and hang out with a harem of women. This is where you become the top 1% of men.

Chapter 18. What is Plate Spinning?

Put simply, plate spinning is a concept that describes how to date and sleep with multiple women at once. In other words, it's a big, fancy word for creating a harem.

The reason why it's called "plate spinning" however, is because it's an apt analogy. Have you ever seen a plate spinner? It's a pretty impressive sight to behold.

It's just a regular guy, who's got a few wooden sticks, and at the very top of each one, there's a glass plate that's spinning. Sometimes, they'll even be spinning 5 or 6 plates at once!

Think of the different women in your life as "plates." Each one is difficult to get started – they require a lot of balance and momentum to get spinning. But, once they get spinning, you don't really have to do much to keep them that way.

The same applies to the women in your life. At first, meeting, attracting, and seducing a woman might be difficult for you. She might put up some resistance, she might test you before fully opening up to you, and she might flat out reject you or ignore you.·

But, once you sleep with her, and get into a consistent ROUTINE of sleeping with her, it's relatively easy to keep this going.

On top of this, once you've got a single plate spinning, you can now focus on getting other plates spinning, since your first plate is spinning of its own accord.

This is the basic idea of "plate spinning." Focus your efforts on getting one fuck buddy at a time, and eventually, your harem will begin to operate by itself for the most part.

Ultimately, this may not be what you want. You may want to find the perfect girlfriend, who you can be loyal to, and who you love unapologetically.

But, until you find this girl, why not have some fun? In fact, what you'll probably come to find out, is that these types of "dream girls" aren't even attracted to men without harems in the first place.

As I've made abundantly clear, women are attracted to men who have "pre-selection." It's a sort of evolutionary shortcut. It takes time for a woman to determine if you're a high-quality man, because she has to screen your behavior, get to know you, and judge your personality.

But, if she knows that you've already slept with a ton of other girls? Well, you must be high value then, right? Those other girls wouldn't do it if you weren't!

This is the power of having a harem. Funny enough, most guys will only find that perfect dream girl, AFTER they've built a harem that satisfies their sexual and emotional needs.

So, with this in mind, how do you build a harem and begin to spin those plates?

Chapter 19. The Iron Rule of Harems

The most important thing to keep in mind, is the iron rule of harems. If you ever, and I mean EVER, break this rule, I will personally find you and smack you across the face.

Okay, are you ready for it? Here we go.

The Iron Rule of Harems is to NEVER brag, and to always be humble.

That's it – that's the rule. It's not to "demonstrate pre-selection," it's not to "be high value," and it's not even to "have good game." No. It's to be fucking humble, and not to brag.

The FIRST thing that you're going to want to do when you gain success with women is BRAG about it...ESPECIALLY to other women! As guys, we think this is the smart thing to do.

After all, women love men who have other women in their lives, right? So, we should tell them, right? WRONG! The first and most important rule of building a harem is to BE HUMBLE.

This cannot be overstated enough. Do not brag, do not be overtly obnoxious, and for the love of God, DO NOT talk about how you're fucking other girls unless it comes up naturally in conversation.

"B-but Jon, why not?" someone might ask...and I'll tell you why. The second that you brag about fucking other women, it sub-communicates two powerful ideas to her:

1. You aren't going to be discreet about her encounter with you.
2. Fucking girls is a big deal for you.

These two things ALONE are enough to drive a woman away from you, and unfortunately, most guys fall victim to this common trap. Again – be humble, do not brag.

When you BRAG about fucking other girls, a woman instantly knows that you will talk about her behind her back. This sets off MASSIVE red flags in her head, because no girl wants to be known as "that slut" who some douche bag is fucking on the side.

Second, bragging about how you fuck girls comes across as try hard. It's not cool, it's not funny, and it's not impressive – it's just annoying. The number one most important aspect of seduction is letting HER put the pieces together.

A woman's imagination is your most powerful ally. If you've done your job right, she will automatically assume that you have a harem and that you're fucking other women. You don't need to go out of your way to tell her this.

Keep it Vague

Of course, if another girl you're sleeping with comes up in conversation, don't get all upset. It's not a big deal so long as you don't mention any NAMES or other identifying factors.

If she ever asks, just AVOID the question. Say things like:

- "Oh, Jessica? Yeah, I know her – we're really good friends."
- "Oh no, it's nothing serious – we're just friends."
- "Nah, we just hang out a lot – we're just friends."

Saying that you're "just friends" with a girl is literally the quintessential line for every fuck boy, and girls KNOW this, but it doesn't matter.

When they know that you can be DISCREET and won't brag and gossip about girls behind their backs, they are 100x more likely to fuck you. ...and what's even more, is that when you say these types of things, you activate a girl's imagination.

Let me give you an example to portray just how powerful this can be.

Back when I wasn't very charming or confident, I managed to sleep with a stunning girl who I will name Emma for the sake of anonymity.

I was probably only fucking 2-3 other girls on the side, but by the way that I acted vague, Emma probably thought that I was banging 50 other girls on the side.

Every time she'd see me text a girl, even if it was COMPLETELY innocent, Emma would assume that I was fucking this girl.

She'd see me nod at a bartender I know, and assume we were fucking. Literally every single interaction I had with a girl was interpreted in the best way possible.

This was despite the fact that I had absolutely piss poor game, but because I knew how to play it vague, Emma's imagination did what it does best: fantasize about a man.

Because I'd slept with Emma, she assumed that I must've been sleeping with hundreds of other women. Why? Because no girl wants to be a slut.

So, what goes through Emma's mind? "Wow, I slept with Jon the first night I met him...so all these other girls that are WAY SLUTTIER than I am must be absolutely throwing themselves at Jon's feet!" This is the power of the hamster.

As a side note, you don't have to outright deny that you're sleeping with a girl, either. Again, just keep it vague. Say things like "Yeah we're just friends," and "Oh yeah, nah it's nothing serious."

Girls will eat this stuff up and immediately assume that you're fucking the girl in question.

Chapter 20. How to Build a Harem

With this "Iron Rule of Harems" in mind, let's now discuss how to build a harem. Building a harem, and getting the "plates spinning" if you will, can be thought about methodically.

First off, you need to have enough LEADS coming into your life. If you're not even meeting any new women to begin with, you can't start to spin any plates.

That means that building a harem is advanced stuff. Even so, it doesn't have to be complicated.

Over the past several years, as I've taught hundreds of men across the globe, I've found that building a good, high-quality harem, comes down to four critical steps:

1. The Pull
2. Retention
3. Repetition
4. Filtration

Beyond this, there's a fifth stage which focuses on building social proof and setting up systems that will naturally slide women into your life.

For now, though, let's focus on the first four stages. "The Pull" will mainly consist of meeting a girl, attracting her, and sleeping with her. For many guys, this will be the hardest stage, but fret not, because we will go in depth here.

"Retention" refers to whether or not she stays in y our life and continues to fuck you. In my experience, if you give a girl good sex, about 50% will come back for at least one more lay.

20% may end up being multi-month fuck buddies, and only about 5-10% will be long term harem members. These numbers may change depending on your preferences and how well you target your women, but over my 150+ lays I've found this number to be true.

"Repetition" refers to simply repeating "The Pull" and increasing your "Retention Rates" which I will give you tips to do. From here, you will eventually move onto the "Filtration" phase.

This is where you begin to actually build the harem that you WANT. It's where you start to pick and choose the women you want to keep seeing, and now that you're coming from abundance, you can truly begin to experience what it's like to own and manage a harem.

Step 1. The Pull

The first step of building a harem, is obviously, to start pulling girls. You can't build a harem if you don't even know how to meet, attract, and seduce women.

That's why this section is more advanced, and in all honesty, you should probably skip it if you haven't yet gotten good at pulling women from scratch.

As I discussed before, there are basically five ways to meet women:

1. Night Game
2. Day Game
3. Social Circle Game
4. Online Dating
5. Social Media

The most effective and efficient ways will vary depending on your own unique style of game, but for me personally, I prefer Night Game, Social Circle Game, and Online Dating.

Once you get in the habit of pulling, you can begin to focus on the next stage of building a harem, which is the Retention stage.

Step 2. Retention

Your retention rate is one of the highest ROI things you can focus on, because it requires so little effort to improve. With just a few tweaks here and there, you can DRASTICALLY increase the amount of sex you're getting on a regular basis, and keep girls coming back for more.

Retention, in a nutshell, comes down to just three things:

1. Having Chemistry
2. Giving Her Good Sex
3. Offering Value

The first, which is having chemistry, is largely up to chance. You will obviously have some chemistry with a girl that you fuck, otherwise you wouldn't be able to fuck her in the first place.

That being said, some girls won't have enough chemistry with you to stick around. Sometimes, you'll only have enough chemistry to have sex once, or maybe just twice, but that's it.

The other two aspects of retention, however, are the most important, because you can quickly and easily change these if you're lacking in them.

The biggest thing is you'll want to give her INCREDIBLE sex. I hope that you purchased my "Ultimate Sex Guide" because it's jam-packed with all of the epic, no-holds-barred tips that you need to make her squirt like a water fountain and scream like a porn star.

If you didn't though, no worries – I'll offer some tips here. To provide her with great sex, get good at using the DEVI method – also known as the Sex God Method.

Admittedly, this will take some practice, but it's worth it to get good at sex. Most guys can't make a girl orgasm, let alone squirt, so if you can learn to do these things, she'll be BEGGING for more.

If you REALLY want to get an edge in the bedroom, consider taking some of natural male enhancement supplements. Supplements like sunflower lecithin, Kratom, and Maca root will cause you to blow 3x bigger loads and last 3x as long.

Just giving a girl incredible sex will make her 99% likely to keep coming back for more. Most guys are terrible in bed, so if you can ace this part, your harem will build itself.

In addition to giving her good sex however, there's one more aspect I want to touch upon – and that's offering value. Generally speaking, there are three types of value:

1. Social Value
2. Lifestyle Value
3. Emotional Value

If you can provide her with any of these, or better yet, all three of them, the odds that she'll keep coming back to fuck you and date you are virtually 100%.

To offer a girl social value, you simply invite her to things and connect her to people. Bring her out to parties or go clubbing with her – this is a great way to add some pre-selection on your side and stack the deck in your favor.

Far too many guys think that you have to "hit it and quit it," but this is absurd. If you get along with a girl, and she gives you great sex, why not prolong the relationship? Why not continue to hang out with her, and do fun things together? Anything else would be stupid.

Offer her lifestyle value by bringing her to travel with you – I personally love doing this. Every now and then I'll choose the #1 girl in my harem and take her on a trip with me to somewhere fun like New York City, Las Vegas, or Miami. This makes her feel special, and in a way, she is.

Lifestyle value can also be given in more simple ways, say hosting women when they travel to you. The girl I previously mentioned (Emma) lives in South Africa.

Even though she's not technically part of my harem anymore, I've offered to have her stay at my place when she's in the states next. In return, she's offered to host me in South Africa.

Doing things like this with women you've fucked is a great way to establish mutually beneficial relationships. I know that when we meet up next, we're going to have great sex and have tons of fun – there's nothing to lose.

Lastly, be sure to offer her EMOTIONAL value. This is by far the most important aspect of offering value, because it costs NOTHING, and it means so much.

To add maximum emotional value, simply spike her emotions when she's with you. Give her the full range of emotions, again – and take her out on Fun Dates™ the Jon Anthony way.

Step 3. Repetition

Once you've got your pulling and your retention down, you want to simply repeat what it is you're already doing, to keep getting results. This phase is pretty simple.

Always keep Tinder installed, no matter what. It doesn't matter if you're fucking 7 playboy bunnies at once – do not uninstall your dating applications.

Never stop going out. Always stay sharp – this is a lesson that I've learned many times over, and it's served me well to adhere to it. It will serve you well to do the same.

As you start to build a harem, you'll want to LEVERAGE this to your advantage. This will be covered more in depth later, but for now, keep it in mind.

Always be sure to MAINTAIN the girls you are sleeping with. Again, this cannot be overstated ENOUGH! It's 100x easier to maintain a girl that you're already fucking than it is to go out and meet a new girl, fuck her, and keep her interested long enough to keep coming back.

The same concept applies to business. It's FAR easier to maintain your current customers than it is to go out and find entirely new ones.

Like I always say, running a harem is like running a well-oiled business – you need to approach it with the exact same mindset, because both cost you time.

Step 4. Filtration

Once you have a harem established, and you've gotten good at maintaining it, the fun begins.

Now you can actually start to pick and choose which women you want in your harem, like a boss. Say that you're fucking ten girls, for example. Two of them are absolutely stunning, six of them are pretty, and two of them are reliable, but not very attractive.

What would you do? In a situation like this, you should start to phase out the less attractive women and focus more on the six pretty girls. Maybe start focusing more on the top 4 most beautiful girls in your harem – the other girls will feel this, and begin to chase you even more.

This will improve your confidence (and thus your game), leading to an upward spiral. Use this to then get more pretty women into your harem, and eventually, you'll go through a process of filtration. Over time, you'll begin to slowly up the quality of the women in your harem.

While you may start out with a few 5's and a single 6, you will eventually graduate up to having a full-blown harem of 10's. This is how Hugh Hefner did it, it's how Dan Bilzerian did it, and it's how I did it. Everyone starts off with a not-so-pretty harem, but hey – can you really complain?

I'd rather have a harem of decent women than no women at all, and I'd think you would, too.

Generally speaking, you can filter for a few things, but most guys will want to focus on just two.

The first of which is obvious: looks. You aren't building a harem to have a business mastermind group, you're building it to fuck lots of pretty girls. So obviously, you can filter based off of looks.

Second, and in my opinion just as important, is filtering based off of PERSONALITY. This is indeed a high-quality problem, but let me tell you – fucking a girl that's hot, but dysfunctional can be a fucking TRAINWRECK for your life.

Don't believe me? You're a fool. Millions of men have had their lives RUINED by letting the wrong woman in. You don't even have to look far – hell, you don't even have to look wide, either. You don't even have to look past the author of this book, because it's happened to me.

Just take a look at the news lately, and what will you see? Dozens of rich, powerful men being BROUGHT DOWN by nasty women. It happened to Kobe Bryant, it happened to Arnold Schwarzenegger, it happened to Brendan Fraser, and it can happen to you.

The wrong girl in your life can WREAK HAVOC on your finances, your emotional health, and your physical health – take my word for it.

With that in mind, there's usually a few things I recommend guys start to filter out:

1. Girls that are drama queens
2. Girls that are bitchy and toxic
3. Girls that just aren't your type

As a man, you always want to be in 100% control of your life... and while "crazy girls" might be fun in bed, they will inevitably destroy your life if you let them. Cut them out, trust me. We will talk more about red flags in "Part 7," but for now understand that you want to eventually start screening the girls in your harem, and kicking the toxic girls out.

Part 7: How Women Should Fit into Your Life

"Every man knows that his highest purpose in life cannot be reduced to any particular relationship. If a man prioritizes his relationship over his highest purpose, he weakens himself, disserves the universe, and cheats his woman of an authentic man who can offer his full, undivided presence."

-David Deida

"Women are an extra."

-Richard Cooper, *Entrepreneurs in Cars*

Executive Summary

First, you want to define your goal. Define exactly what it is that you want from a woman. What do you want her to look like, what do you want her to be like, and how do you want her to fit into your life? Defining your goal is important, because without first defining your goal, you won't even know what it is you're trying to attain.

Once you define your goal, you can learn how and where to find your ideal woman. This part of dating is known as "demographics." For instance, if you're looking to meet a lot of sexy, party girls, who just want to have fun, you will probably meet these girls by doing night game at raves, festivals, at bars, and at nightclubs.

If, on the other hand, you want to meet conservative women who are interested in starting a family, then doing so through day game at coffee shops, grocery stores, malls, and through conservative religious groups, churches, etc., will probably be your best bet.

Much of this process, of finding the perfect woman who fits into your life exactly how you want her to, entails screening. For screening, I typically look for red flags, but in addition to this, I also look for several green flags.

Red flags are not necessarily a "make or break" type deal, although some of them are. If a girl is exceptionally hot, I may put up with a red flag or two, but I do not fool myself. If she has too many red flags, the odds that she will be loyal and will have a net positive on your life are extremely low. Girls with a lot of red flags are good for one thing, and one thing only: sex.

Typical red flags include things like she has a high notch count, frequently complains, mocks masculine men, and has a bad relationship with her father. I have provided a fairly extensive list in this Part, so you may want to take notes.

In addition to this, I discuss something that's often overlooked, which is GREEN flags. Many men focus on the red flags, but in my experience, it's not just the absence of red flags that make a girl worthy of long-term commitment. It's also the presence of green flags.

In other words, it's not enough that she just doesn't mock masculinity (which if she did, would be a red flag). She should also CELEBRATE it (which is a green flag), and cherish masculine men, for serving our community.

Again, these screening flags are typically only necessary when it comes to a longer-term relationship, but once you develop enough of a harem, and enough game, you will apply them to most of the women you meet, regardless of how hot they are.

Chapter 21. Defining Your Goal

As you begin to date more and more women, and as you start to develop the skillset to become more attractive with women, it's time to ask yourself: what do you really want?

Most men are happy with just fucking a lot of different girls at first, but will eventually want a long-term relationship, to offer a deeper connection than any fuckbuddy could ever give.

I'd urge you to take some time to think about what you REALLY want out of your dating life. Do you want to just bang a bunch of girls for now? Do you want to find an awesome girlfriend?

Whatever it is that you want, my friend, you can have it. You just have to be willing to create a plan and execute on it, until you get what it is that you so desperately desire.

Let's refer to the questions I asked in Part 3:

1. What does your perfect 10 look like?
2. How tall is she?
3. How much does she weigh?
4. What color eyes does she have?
5. What color hair?
6. What is her body type?
7. What is her personality like?
8. Is she shy or outgoing?
9. Is she adventurous or reserved?

Take some time to really think about what it is you want from a girl, because I promise you, at some point, you will crave a long-term relationship.

While it might sound nice, fucking a lot of girls is not all it's cracked up to be. Take my word for it, I've been there, and if you don't spend time cultivating close relationships with friends, family, and a girlfriend, you will feel incredibly empty inside.

Again though, I want to be clear. I'm not saying I'm against sleeping with a lot of women – in fact, I'm anything but. Still, though, it's important to keep the "bigger picture" in mind.

Do you want to have a family at some point? Good, then use the tools in this book to find your dream girl. Woo her, make her fall in love with you, and have your children with her.

If you're a younger guy, perhaps you want to play the field. You can do that as well. It's entirely up to you, my friend – again, it's your life, and you can do whatever you want to do.

Chapter 22. Finding Your Ideal Woman

Something that isn't talked about NEARLY as much as it should be in the dating world, is the demographics aspect of meeting women.

Demographics are simply where you tend to meet what type of women. Once you understand this simple concept, finding your perfect 10 will actually be quite easy.

For example, are you looking to "play the field" and sleep with lots of women? You're probably looking for girls who are "down to fuck" and are just looking to have fun.

Where do you think the best place to find these types of girls would be? Out at night clubs and bars, of course. While this may seem obvious, you would be shocked at how many men fail to realize this simple truth.

You're generally going to find shy, intellectual girls, in bookstores. You'll probably find fit chicks at the gym, hippie girls at raves, and conservative girls at church.

Again, these things seem extremely obvious, but most men don't ever even begin to internalize the simple facts of demographics.

So, with this in mind, ask yourself: "What type of girl am I looking for?" Then, once you figure this question out, ask yourself: "Where can I find her?"

If you really like black chicks, consider moving to an area with a lot of black chicks. If you like Russian models, consider moving to Kiev. If you enjoy strong, business-minded women, move to Manhattan and master the art of day game.

Once you start to connect the dots, and realize that finding your dream girl isn't actually that hard, you will be shocked at how you failed to recognize this earlier.

Chapter 23. Screening Women

Learning to screen women properly is one of the most important skillsets that you will ever learn. The reason being that, simply put, you do NOT want a crazy girl in your life!

I've seen many good men get destroyed by a toxic, manipulative woman, and as sad as it is to say this, many men never fully recover.

The good news is, that if you've picked up this book, you're willing to learn the truth – at all costs. And so, with that in mind, I'd like to talk about screening women.

The first thing to understand, is that what you screen for depends precisely on what you're looking for. Not all screening will look the same.

For example, if you're just looking for a one-night stand, you probably don't care too much about her personality. Sure, maybe if she's batshit crazy you'll ditch her, but chances are if she's hot, then she fits the bill.

If, on the other hand, you're thinking of letting her into your life, and potentially dating her, then you're DEFINITELY going to want to screen her... HARD.

In my opinion, there are a few major "red flags" that certain women will give off, that are pretty much a deal-breaker for me. I MIGHT make an exception for a one-night stand, if she's exceptionally hot, but aside from that, I offer a firm "no."

In addition to "red flags" however, there are also "green flags." These are things that she might do or say, that are actually a good sign that she'll be good LTR material.

Screening women is primarily used to determine whether they will be a good girlfriend or not, so the list is pretty extensive and unforgiving. Here it is:

- Has a high partner count
- Frequently complains
- Nothing is ever her fault
- Always talks about how she was "raped"
- Has tattoos and/or body piercings
- Always seems to find drama in her life
- Willing to flirt with or fuck you even though she has a boyfriend
- Frequently makes excuses not to have sex
- Constantly posting on social media
- Addicted to her smartphone
- Doesn't clean or cook, despite living with you for free
- Physically strikes you in any manner that isn't playful
- Ex-boyfriends are all abusive assholes
- Has a swarm of beta orbiters
- Doesn't have a good relationship with her family
- Mocks masculinity, isn't grateful for men
- Has an entitlement complex
- Dumps her emotional baggage on you
- Constantly talks about "women's issues"
- Passive aggressive
- Gets defensive when you tease her
- Feels the need to compete with you
- Any sort of addiction
- Never takes responsibility

...and, of course, the biggest red flag of them all: she has a bad relationship with her father.

If a woman has a bad relationship with her father, she is almost 100% of the time, not going to be good long-term relationship material.

This doesn't mean you need to hate her. To be fair, maybe her dad was an asshole – but that is going to cause a shit ton of emotional problems that you do NOT want to deal with, my friend.

I know this list is pretty harsh... in fact, there's probably a special someone who you're thinking of, and you're wondering why she has a few of those items.

Keep in mind that this list is ONLY really if you're trying to screen HARD for a long-term relationship to have children with.

This is not a list for screening fuckbuddies, or girls who you just want to date and have fun with.

But it's essential you are aware of these things, because if you ever want to find a good girl in today's modern world, it's going to be pretty fucking difficult.

Green Flags

In addition to red flags, there's also green flags. These are behaviors and activities that a woman might do, that show you she's got good girlfriend/LTR material.

While green flags don't necessarily cancel out red flags, they can certainly be a good indicator of a girl who's at least trying to improve, and who could be a good girlfriend.

Here's a comprehensive list of green flags:

- Has a good relationship with her father
- Takes accountability for her actions
- Eager to please you sexually

- Doesn't use alcohol or drugs
- Takes good care of her body
- Respectful to waiters/waitresses
- Has a clean/organized room
- Can cook well
- Spends time reading, not on social media
- Optimistic
- Good sense of humor
- Completely debt-free
- Strong family values
- Raised Christian/conservative
- Was homeschooled

In my experience, that last one is probably the BIGGEST green flag of them all. So many girls nowadays learn to be manipulative and toxic from their peer groups in high schools, so if you can find a girl who was homeschooled, the odds she's girlfriend material are pretty high.

In fact, I would go so far as to say that the only girl I ever SERIOUSLY considered marrying was a homeschooled girl. She was sweet, pleasant, submissive, and incredibly fun to be around.

All in all, learning to read between the lines is a skill that you will probably have to develop, but after a little bit of practice, you'll find it isn't that hard.

The biggest thing to look for is her _relationship with her father._ The old cliché rings true… if she's got daddy issues, then she's going to be a nightmare in a relationship.

Part 8: The Iron Rules of Jon

"Love is three quarters curiosity."

-Giacomo Casanova

"Women are attracted to men who have a strong sense of purpose in life, and the second that she senses she can sway you from that purpose, she will recognize you for what you are—a weak little boy, who can be taken off his true path in life by the promise of sex."

-Jon Anthony

Executive Summary

I understand that much of this book is probably overwhelming. Learning to evolve from a blue pilled, average frustrated chump, into an alpha male, in the top 1%, is going to take time. That's why I put together a list of my Iron Rules, so that you can easily start following them, and speed this process of evolution along.

Many of these rules are not only meant to increase her attraction to you, but to keep you safe from toxic women, and to improve your life as a whole. I recommend you read this section many times over, and if you're ever having trouble with a particular woman, come back to this section, and ask yourself which rule you are violating.

The first rule, is to always stay on your purpose. Your purpose must come first, before anything else. Second, is to let her imagination do the work. As I have discussed previously, a woman's imagination is the single biggest thing you should leverage when trying to seduce her.

Third, is to never judge a woman, but to discern instead. Judging people never works – in fact, it often has the exact opposite effect that most people intend. If you ever judge a woman for sleeping around, she will obviously not want to sleep with you. That being said, you should still be discerning. If she sleeps around, don't judge her, but don't make her your girlfriend.

Fourth, is to watch a woman's actions, not her words. Women are experts in indirect communications, rather than direct communications. They might not always tell you exactly what they think, but mark my words, their actions will.

Fifth, is play to your strengths, and re-frame your weaknesses. In your won frame and reality, you should be the top dog. You are

#1 and nobody else. Your weaknesses add color to who you are, and make you more relatable.

Sixth, is to always fuck her good. Period. When you fuck a woman good, you turn on a primal trigger in her brain, that says: "This man is an alpha male. Fall in love with him."

Seventh, is to value her happiness more than your relationship with her. If she is not happy with you, and loses her attraction to you, then leave her. You will both be happier for it.

Eighth, is to make her jealous. This is particularly important when in a longer-term relationship, as using dread game is a great way to spark attraction in your relationship.

Ninth, is to always hold your frame. I don't care what you say, what you do, or what happens. You are in command. You are the alpha male. You can acknowledge when you fuck something up, but NEVER apologize or cave into a woman's demands, simply because she says.

Lastly, is to always have a backup plan. Understand that there is no "one" and if you ever need to, you could easily meet other women to start dating and fucking. This will create confidence in who you are, and feed your abundance mentality.

While I aimed to be as comprehensive as possible in this book, most of what I've already said has probably been forgotten. This is normal.

It takes time for new information to sink in. That's why I recommend most men read and re-read my book at least 10-15 times over the course of the next few years.

...but while the contents of this book may be difficult to remember in their entirety, simple rules are not. In fact, simple rules are very easy to remember.

That's why I've created a list of 10 commandments, which I've dubbed "The Iron Rules of Jon." Under NO CIRCUMSTANCES are you to break ANY of these rules. Ever.

Following these rules will lead to an abundance of women, and high-quality women at that. But if you choose to ignore my warnings, and succumb to your beta inclinations? It will be death.

So, without further ado, let's get started.

Rule 1. Your Purpose Must Always Come First

The very first rule is that your purpose must always come first. Again, it doesn't matter what your purpose is – whether it's to make a million bucks, grow your business empire, or to just enjoy your life. You MUST have a purpose that comes before women.

If you don't, she will not respect you – period. I know this sounds harsh, and believe me, I wish it wasn't true, but it is. Women respect and admire men who are going places. This is hypergamy.

The essence of masculine energy is to go places – it's to have a firm sense of direction, and a strong, unbreakable sense of purpose. When you do this, women will fall in line.

If you make HER your purpose, she will slowly start to resent you for it. When a woman falls in love with a man, it's because he has a strong sense of direction.

She enjoys following his lead. He takes her out to places, he takes the lead in all interactions, and he becomes her emotional anchor.

When that anchor starts to waver, however – in other words, when he loses his sense of direction and purpose – she will lose attraction for you.

Unfortunately, most men don't understand this. They spend their entire lives dedicating their purpose to women, and the consequences are, without exaggerating, deadly. In my article, entitled: "Why Your Masculine Purpose Should Always Come Before Women," I discuss what happens when men put a woman first:

> *Making women your purpose is nothing short of deadly, and I do not exaggerate when I say this. Making a woman your purpose in life will almost inevitably lead to feelings of*

worthlessness, depression, self-loathing, and sometimes even suicide.

With the dangers that come from making a woman your purpose, you'd think that mainstream society would tell us the truth—however as I'm sure you know by now, the masses prefer a comfortable lie over a painful truth every single time.

Elliot Rodger made women his purpose. Every breathe, every action, every single thought was him asking himself how he could gain more approval from women—and while some level of this is certainly normal, taken to the extreme, it leads to incredible mental sickness.

Women are repulsed when you make them your purpose. Ever wonder why they're so willing to discard a guy who puts her before his own life, meanwhile they chase the guy who barely seems to have time for her? It's because one of them puts his own life's purpose before her, and the other doesn't. Can you guess which is which?

Let me make this crystal clear. As a man, you must NEVER sacrifice your own life, your own priorities, and your own happiness for a woman, even if she's "the one."

Even if you think that you will love her forever, women are flighty and emotional creatures, and chances are she will unconsciously begin to test you at some point.

Typically, women don't even have to test your sense of direction or purpose. Most men make it crystal clear that she's their #1 priority in life.

Most men immediately drop all plans when a girl asks to hang out, and are _way too easy_ to nail down. Women like a challenge. They want a man who is busy with his own life.

Make it your priority to build a better life – even if it's something as simple as making a few hundred extra bucks a month, or going out once a week on a fishing trip.

Whatever it is, you need to be in control of your own happiness, your own life, and your own purpose. If you are not, many women will ruthlessly manipulate you and discard you.

This doesn't mean to be paranoid, however. In fact, I personally LOVE how women are attracted to men with a strong purpose. How could you not?

Imagine for a second, that you, as a man, get to focus 100% on making your own life awesome. You get to focus all of your energy on making tons of money, picking up chicks for one-night stands, and having a bunch of fun, awesome hobbies.

On top of this, women will literally chase YOU. They will reach out to you, text you first, send you risky pictures, and call you on Friday nights. How could you not love this setup?

It takes some time to get used to this, but once you make the shift and put your own purpose and life first, you'll realize how incredibly supportive feminine energy can be.

Rule 2. Let Her Imagination Do The Work

The second Iron Rule is to always let her imagination do the work. As a man, you never want to spill all of your cards on the table. You want to make her wonder.

Often times, I'm asked what the most potent seduction tool is. Perhaps it's to get her qualifying? Or maybe it's push/pull game? Witty banter? What is it?

In reality, your biggest "seduction tool" is actually a woman's _own imagination._ When you learn to use a woman's fantasy to your advantage, your dating life will literally 10x.

Let me give you an example...

I was out with a girl a while back, and we were hanging out at this hookah bar. I knew the bartender there, so I decided to get up from our table and just say hi to her for a minute.

The second I went back to see the girl I was with, she asked: "Have you fucked her before?" It was clear that she was intensely filled with jealousy.

"No, of course not," I said. She didn't believe me. In her mind, she knew me as the "player," and because of that, every single girl I talked to was probably fucking me.

Within minutes, she was sucking my dick in the bathroom. I'm not saying this to be crass, crude, or to brag, but to illustrate the power of a woman's imagination.

When a girl likes you, she will literally grow wet thinking about you. She will wake up thinking about you, go to sleep thinking about you, and when she's sleeping, she will dream about you.

What's funny too is you don't even have to be 10% the man she thinks you are. You just have to be "cool enough" and learn how to let her imagination doing the work.

Use the advice I gave you previously in "Part 6: Plate Spinning," where I talked about being vague and never explicitly stating that you've fucked a girl.

When you blatantly say: "Yeah, I fucked her," women will not only view you as indiscreet, but they will no longer wonder about you anymore.

Keep it vague. Don't give straight answers. It's not uncommon that I don't tell a girl what I do for a living until I've already slept with her. I reward women in bits and pieces.

For example, I met a girl on Tinder several days ago, and she asked me what I do. After my initial "I sell drugs and do porn" joke, she kept asking me. So, I revealed a little bit.

"I have a YouTube channel," I said. "What is it?" she asked. "Haha, I'm not telling. But maybe we can watch one of my videos when we hang out later," I said.

Do you see the beauty in this? As she's talking to me, she will be filled with wonder. This feeling of intrigue and curiosity might start off as a small spark, but eventually, you can fan it into a fire.

Rule 3. Never Judge Women (But Discern)

The third Iron Rule, is to never judge women... but rather to discern them. As a whole, you should never judge people. Not because it isn't "fair" of course – some people are terrible human beings, and we can say this objectively.

The thing is though, judging doesn't teach you anything. You can't learn why someone did something if all you say is "wow, what a bitch!" Instead of judging, DISCERN. Yes, maybe someone is a toxic individual, but ask yourself WHY they did this, and learn from it.

When a girl flakes on you, refuses to sleep with you, or cheats on you, use it as a learning experience.

I was grabbing a beer with a friend recently, and he told me about his new life philosophy that he'd been trying to uphold. "Lately, I've let go of judging people... it's not that they did something wrong, it's that my expectations of them weren't accurate."

Gentlemen, this is the best way to approach women (and life) as a whole. When you judge a woman, you never learn anything about her, you just peg her as "bad" or as "a slut."

In addition to this, _ANY TIME_ people feel like you're judging them, they will immediately lock up and view you as an enemy. Even your closest friends – if you begin to act judgmental towards them, it won't be long before they stop sharing intimate details about themselves with you.

The same can be said about women. When I'm with a girl, I make it a point to NEVER judge her. Even if she tells me the craziest, most ridiculous stories – and because of this, women trust me. When you don't judge women, they view you as one of the "cool guys."

Most guys are incredibly judgmental of a woman's sexuality. They judge her for all sorts of things – for sleeping with other guys, for having threesomes, and everything else.

So, do you think a girl is going to want to be sexual around the type of guy who literally JUDGES her for being sexual? Of course not! Why would she?

Take me, on the other hand. I'll routinely ask girls what their craziest sexual experience was, and I'll cheer them on as they're telling it. I've had girls tell me stories that would make your hair curl. Stories that they would probably never tell anyone else.

But, why do they tell me? Because I don't judge them.

The other day, a girl told me about how she used to do porn. Did I judge her? Of course not. I know that if I start judging her for this, she won't open up to me anymore.

Now, here's the key – even though you should never judge a woman, you must always be DISCERNING of women. This is a critical difference.

If a woman tells me that she did porn, will I judge her? Of course not. But do you think I'll make a mental note of it, and think to myself: "Hmm... she's probably not LTR material."

Of course, I will! You would be a fool to never use discernment. As a man in today's modern world, you absolutely must discern between different types of women.

Anytime a woman shows you one of the red flags that I listed in Part 7? Make a note of it. If she mentions a ton of crazy sex stories, make a note of it.

You don't have to judge her – but don't be stupid. If she's the type of girl who regularly sucks the bartender's dick to get a free drink, you probably don't want to be exclusive with her.

Rule 4. Listen to What A Woman Does, Not What She Says

One of the biggest mistakes I see men making is that they judge women by their words, and not by their actions. Take, for example, setting up a date.

I've had clients of mine get flaked on by a woman multiple times. She says that she wants to meet with them, but every time the date they set up rolls around, she's a no show.

"B-but she told me her dog's cousin's uncle died, and she had to go to the funeral!" they'll tell me. Girls always have an excuse if they aren't interested.

When a woman isn't interested in you, she'll typically "tell you" with her actions, not with her words. Women are often afraid of how a man will react if they flat out tell him they're not interested, so they often resort to simply flaking on him, or ghosting him altogether.

If she says she's interested in going on a date with you, but then never responds to your texts, she isn't actually interested in going on a date with you.

If she says she was busy, but then doesn't offer a different time and date to meet you in return, then she probably doesn't want to meet you that much in the first place.

Learning to read a woman's actions above and beyond all else, is critical. Once you start employing this advice, you'll notice just how many women were lying to you.

This is a good thing, though. Once you pick up on these small signs, you can stop texting women who aren't interested in you, and one of two things will happen:

1. They'll leave altogether
2. They'll come running back

If they don't fight to stay in your life, then good – they didn't even want to be there in the first place. You just saved yourself a ton of wasted time and energy that you can now focus on women who actually give a damn about you.

If they come running back, then good. You know she's into you, and wants to be a part of your life. I recommend you try not sending out a SINGLE text for a week, and see who texts you first.

The results will be enlightening.

Rule 5. Play to Your Strengths, Re-Frame Your Weaknesses

So much of game is in the frame... If your frame is strong, and you are confident in who you are, a woman will naturally view you as an alpha male, and will fall in love with you.

This is why you must become a master at brainwashing yourself. Anytime something "bad" happens, or you have some "weakness," portray it as a strength, or ignore it altogether.

Say, for example, you drive a Toyota Corolla. You're with a girl, and she talks about how you should get a "Lamborghini," or some other exotic car.

In some sense, is it a weakness that you can't afford a $500,000 car? Of course, it is. But, should you frame it as a weakness? Of course, you shouldn't.

Instead, frame it as: "I'm being responsible and budgeting. That's what a smart man does."

That's all you need to say. Anything that is supposedly a "weakness" can be turned into a positive thing, if you know how to use your frame the right way.

When I was in college, I drove a shitty used car, but I was proud of it. When I saw someone driving around in the BMW or Porsche that their daddy bought them, do you think I got upset?

A little bit, yeah. But did I let it last long? Of course not. My frame was: "Wow, what a bitch. That guy's riding off of his father's coattails. What a pussy. I'm going to surpass him in just a few years, and he's going to be a weak loser by then."

Would I have liked to have had a BMW or a Porsche? Obviously. But if you don't have the means to achieve something yet, why not re-frame it into a positive?

In some sense, anything can be a positive if you learn how to frame it properly. Let's take a closer look at the "making money" vs. "pulling chicks" dichotomy.

If I'm making a ton of money, and killing it at business, what do you think my frame is? It's something along the lines of:

"God, I'm such a boss. Women love me, because I'm a stud who's self-employed. How many guys have the balls to start a business? Not many. Girls love me when I'm on my purpose... fuck yeah. I'm the shit. I'm so cool. Look at how much money I made today, man. I can use it to buy an awesome life and eventually provide for a family."

While it might sound comical and ridiculous, these things actually go through my head when I'm in the zone. Am I perfect? Of course not. Do I have flaws? Of course.

I have plenty of flaws that I work on daily. Sometimes people will confuse my confidence with arrogance, but the fact is I probably do more as a person to improve myself than 99% of others.

It's ultimately a paradox. Acknowledge that you're not perfect, but that you're still the shit for being exactly who you are. Girls love you for who you are. Repeat this phrase 1,000 times.

Even if my business came crumbling to the ground, I went $500,000 in debt, and became broke and hungry, my frame would still be positive:

"FUCK I'm such a god damn boss. Look at me – out here living life and taking risks. In 10 years, I'm going to look back and thank these hard times for making me who I am. Look at that pretentious pussy over there in his nice ass car. What a weak little bitch – I'm out here taking the bus every day, waiting in the 20-degree weather... I'm fucking

209

tough, man. He's weak. Everyone else is weak. Those who hustle stay humble."

When you learn to develop this level of frame control, you will find that women will naturally fall into your reality. People naturally follow the most confident person in the room, and if you're continually re-framing your own reality to suit you, that person will be you.

Rule 6. Always Fuck Her Good

One of the most important things in a relationship, of any kind, is to always fuck her good. I don't care if you never think you'll see her again – fuck her brains out like a porn star.

The way I see it is this… most guys are horrible in bed. They only last a few minutes, can't finger a girl, can't make her squirt, and can barely create any sexual chemistry.

On top of this, most girls only sleep with a new guy a couple of times a year. So, if you can literally just give her good sex (not even great sex), she will do 90% of the pursuing.

This tip is going to seem obvious. It's going to seem like a no brainer. "No shit, Jon – obviously I want to give a girl good sex." But trust me, you won't realize how important this is until you've been in this game for a few years.

I remember when I first got started in pickup, I was solely focused on racking up lays. I wanted to get 10 lays, then 20, then 30… but I started noticing something.

So, few of the girls I slept with would ever come around again. That meant if I wanted to get laid regularly, I literally had to go out every night of the week to find a new girl.

It wasn't until a few years later, that I realized if you just focus on RETENTION (discussed in Part 6: Plate Spinning) you can get so much bang for your buck.

Think about it… which one is better:

1. Put in 3+ hours to meet, attract, and seduce a woman, and then never have her come back, so you're left with your dick in your hands all the time
2. Put in 3+ hours to meet her, but then fuck her really well, and see her each week

211

Obviously, option number two is the best. To meet new girls, you have to put in a lot of investment upfront – but if you just put in a little bit of effort in the bedroom, all of a sudden, you can start having regular sex, and developing a much better intimate relationship.

Another reason you want to fuck a girl well, is if you can do this, she will naturally fall in love with you faster, and submit to you as a man.

It sounds strange, but when you can give a girl incredible, dominant, world-shattering sex, she will naturally think to herself: "Wow, this guy must be an alpha male."

Sex is an art, and there's really no way to get good at it without practicing. That being said, I urge you to re-read "Part 6: Plate Spinning" because it's just that important.

Always fuck her good. When you do this, she will come back for more, time and time again.

Rule 7. Value Her Happiness More Than Your Relationship With Her

Whenever you're with a girl, whether she's just a fuckbuddy, or a girlfriend of 10 years, you must value her happiness more than your own relationship with her.

Why is this? Because, if she senses that you want to maintain the relationship at all costs, because you're *afraid of losing her*, she will lose attraction.

This rule is sort of a sneaky way of saying: "Never grow too needy," and when you follow this rule, you'll grow non-needy in a sort of roundabout way.

Think about it... if you value her own happiness, more than her relationship with you, what will you do if she starts arguing and throwing temper tantrums?

You'll let her loose. You might tell her something like: "Baby, I really love you, but if you're unhappy with me, then I think you need to go. I love you and wish you the best."

Cultivating this type of attitude will not only increase her attraction for you (because non-possessiveness communicates abundance), but it is also the healthiest thing you can do.

Understand that if she isn't happy with you, then it's time to let her go. When a woman is satisfied with her man, she will make him happy – in this case, she will make you happy.

But when she's not? She will make his world hell. She will throw temper tantrums, passively resist him, and actively do things to spite him. This will ruin your life if you let it. In fact, having my life ruined by women before was one of the best lessons I ever learned.

Why? Because it taught me to be a fucking man, and to stop putting up with bullshit. The second I realize someone is going to pose a problem in my life, and proactively mess with my ability to stay focused, I cut them out. Period.

The Universe will continually throw distractions and bullshit at you, until you learn this lesson, and develop the ability to form strong boundaries.

The most important thing in a long-term relationship is to balance your love and affection for her, with a healthy amount of non-neediness and indifference to her state.

As I've said before, there are many paradoxes within human relationships. On the one hand, you want to care for her, appreciate her, desire her, and love her. But on the other, you must also be willing to let her go if she would be happier without you.

Rule 8. Make Her Jealous

As I've said before, nothing excites a woman more than knowing other women are interested in you. Women love it when their man is desired by other women. It makes them feel special.

Now, I know what you're thinking. A common problem guys often have, is when they first learn these concepts, they go _too far in the opposite direction._

Take, for example, the following reader question that I got a few weeks ago:

> *"Hey, Jon. I've been reading your blog for two years now, and it's completely changed my life. Everything from your morning routine to your Body of an Alpha book is completely amazing. I just have one question. I've been seeing this girl for a while, and I've been making her jealous like you say... and while she seems to like it, she also seems to get really upset by it. Can you give me any advice on what to do?"*

This is one of the more common questions that I get, and the solution is actually pretty simple.

As I said before, you have to balance your love and affection for her, with your willingness to let her go if need be. In this reader's question, one of two things is wrong:

1. He's not giving her enough attention to make her feel special
2. She's simply insecure and has low self-esteem

While you must ALWAYS make it clear to your woman that other women want you, and that you are a high-value man, you must also make it clear that she's special and that you chose her.

The reason why is because it isn't just being a high-value man that women want. A woman's ultimate fantasy is to find a high-value man, and SEDUCE HIM into a relationship, even though he has literally dozens of other options that he could be sleeping with.

As I've said before, nothing is more validating for a woman than this. When she knows that she was CHOSEN amongst many, she feels incredibly special, because it means something.

This is why, in conjunction with using "dread game" you must also woo her. Take her out on regular "fun dates" each week. Break your dull routine. Do something enjoyable with her.

Familiarity and boredom are the death of passion, and the true master pickup artist understands how to balance enough familiar intimacy with enough new passion.

The other problem, is that she might just have low self-esteem. When a woman is confident in herself, she doesn't mind that other women want you – in fact, it actually turns her on.

The same can be said for a man, as well. When my woman is looking all sexy and beautiful, and I take her out to the club, I love watching other guys eye her and try to hit on her.

Why? Not because I have some weird cuck fetish, but because I like knowing that despite all these guys wanting her, she wants me. Later that night, I get to take her home and fuck her, and those other guys don't.

This is how women feel. They want you to flirt (subtly, of course) with the women around them. Flirt with the cute waitress at dinner, flirt with the bartender, flirt with the girls at the gym. Don't be obnoxious, but do it enough that she notices.

This is one of many ways to keep the passion alive in your relationship.

Rule 9. Hold Your Frame

Whenever you're in a relationship with a woman, you must always hold your frame. Never back down, and never apologize for being who you are.

If, for example, I make a joke that a woman finds offensive, I will RARELY ever apologize unless I believe that I said something stupid.

Most of the time, I'll just double down, and amplify the joke. I don't like submitting to a woman's frame. I don't even like submitting to a man's frame.

I don't like it when people tell me what to do, and you shouldn't either. You, as a man, are in charge of your own life – and no boss, no government bureaucracy, and no other human being can order you around without your permission.

The most important thing in a relationship is that you hold your "frame." Frame is simply defined as your underlying set of beliefs; it's your underlying reality.

Let me give you an example. When I hang out with a regular fuck buddy of mine, what do you think the "frame" is? It's really simple:

> *"This girl is lucky to be with me. I could be building my empire, relaxing and reading a book on self-development, or hanging out with a buddy of mine. Instead, I chose to be with her. I want to fuck her good, have fun, spike her emotions, and ultimately, make her feel great when she's hanging around me. We're on my time."*

Can you see how strong this frame is? Let's take a moment to contrast it with a typical frame that most guys have when they go on a date, or hang out with a girl, hoping to sleep with her:

"Wow, she's so pretty. Am I good enough for her? I hope so. Let me turn on the charm and hope that I can get lucky and get her in bed! If I even get a kiss at the door I'll be lucky. Gee, I hope she thinks I'm funny and confident like an alpha male!"

Do you see how weak this frame is? Better yet, can you imagine how a woman will react when a man has a frame like this? Again, she will buy into whoever's frame is stronger.

If you have the frame of "Am I good enough for her?" then she will naturally expect you to jump through her hoops and validate yourself to her.

If you have the frame of: "I'm willing to put in the work to sleep with you, but I want to make sure you're worth it first, and make sure that we have chemistry," then she will respect you.

Even if a girl doesn't want to have sex with you, she will respect you 10,000 times more for taking your shot, than the man who is too cowardly to do so.

Now, this is the critical part of holding your frame. At first, women will typically test your frame to see how strong it is. This is what I mean by "holding the frame."

When a woman tests your frame, you want to hold strong to it. She may say something, do something, or act a certain way, to see how easily your frame can be shaken.

For example, say you've been acting confident and cool with a girl for the past month. She's starting to really like you, and she's enjoying the great sex and deep conversation with you.

Then, all of a sudden, she goes cold. She stops responding to your texts, and you can't for the life of you figure out why. She starts giving you a ton of mixed signals, and you wonder to yourself if she's still even into you anymore. Funny enough, this actually happened to me recently.

What is the best thing to do in this situation? Well first, you must understand that she is *TESTING YOUR FRAME.* Not consciously, of course – but she's testing it nonetheless.

She wants to see if you really are the cool, confident, aloof guy you're portraying yourself to be, so she's throwing out a test to see how you respond.

So, how do you respond? Well, first let me tell you how most guys would respond. They would get upset, blow her phone up with a million calls, and send her messages like the following:

> *"Hey, why the hell haven't you returned my calls? I thought we had something special? What the hell happened, did you find a new boy already? I can't believe you, are you too busy for me now? What's going on?"*

This is DEATH and will destroy her attraction for you. Why? Because in this example, you showed her your true colors. You aren't actually the confident, cool guy she thought you were.

If you really WERE a confident and cool guy, you would understand that women take time to fall in love, and they will often test you – and you would especially NEVER chase women.

So, when she doesn't call you back and ignores you? No worries, you'll just go onto the next girl and give her some space. It doesn't matter to you, because you live in a world of abundance.

Funny enough, as I said before, this actually happened to me. I've been dating and sleeping with a beautiful brunette bombshell, and she suddenly went cold.

Here's what happened, and how I responded. As you read this story, ask yourself what is going through her head when she's testing me, and what is going through MY head:

I met this girl about 7 months ago. She was a beautiful, brown-haired girl, with a body to kill for. She seemed to really like me, and we slept together on the first night.

Over the next few weeks, we texted back and forth, and slept together a few more times. She was very warm and receptive, and would send me naughty pictures of herself. She would tell me things like: "I can't wait to see you again!" and "You should come visit me when I go back to college, and spend the night!"

Then, all of a sudden, she stopped responding to me. Not a single word. I never got angry or needy, though. At most, maybe I was a little bit confused, but that was it. I understood that she was busy, and that she probably wanted some space.

So, I sent her a funny meme or two on Instagram, which was something that we always did, and after getting no response, that was that. I figured she would reply if she wanted to, so I decided to focus on my own life and get my own shit handled.

I did notice, however, that she kept watching my Snapchat and Instagram stories, so she still had some interest in me. Again though, I didn't respond.

Then, after about two months of complete radio silence, she texted me out of the blue.

"Does this relate to you?" she asked me. She had sent me a text message, linking to an article on how a popular cryptocurrency exchange had been hacked. She knew I taught guys how to trade cryptocurrencies, so it was clear she sent it to me specifically.

I told her: "Haha, nah. I don't keep my money on sketchy exchanges. Thanks for thinking of me, though!" and that was that. I didn't try to eagerly compliment her, chase her, ask if I could come down and visit her, or anything.

Then, she liked one of the memes I sent her on Instagram a few months ago, to show me that she saw it. This was her way of saying: "Hey, I'm sorry I didn't respond to your message before, but you're still on my radar!"

Very soon after, she sent me another risqué picture of her in lingerie, and asked if I wanted to come visit her for the night. I told her I'd love to come visit sometime, but that I was busy. "Let me call you when I'm more available," I said.

Again, I didn't jump right into her frame, because as I said, I was genuinely focused on my own life. About two weeks later, I called her. We set up a weekend for me to come down, which I followed through on, and when I was there, I banged her all night long.

She was 100% into me, and she still is.

I know that was probably a little bit too detailed for your taste, but really examine how this story relates to holding your frame when a woman shit tests you.

At NO POINT during the interaction did I chase her. Yes, I took the initiation to set up the dates and times to meet, but that's not the same as chasing her.

As a man, you should pursue women, but NEVER chase them. "Pursuing" means setting up the date. "Chasing" means continually blowing up her phone, calling her, and texting her, even when she's giving you zero interest in return.

I made it clear – I want to meet you, and I want to fuck you, and I want to hang out and have a good time with you. But I'm not the type of guy who will shower you in endless compliments and give you endless attention when you don't return my messages.

This is an excellent example of a _LONG-TERM SHIT TEST_. This is a term that I have coined (you heard it here first), to describe how women test your frame over longer periods of time.

Women are always testing to see how strong your frame is, and often with the most attractive women, if there's even a 1% waver in your frame, they will lose attraction for you.

Let me list a few ways that women will shit test your frame. As you're reading this list, ask yourself how many women have done this to you, and how you responded:

- Ignore you
- Go hot and cold
- Get angry at you
- Flirt with other guys in front of you
- Stop you from going to the gym
- Throw temper tantrums
- Pout when they didn't get their way

These are all various versions of a shit test, and as a test of your frame. Again, don't think that women do these things consciously thinking they want to test your frame. They don't.

But, they do them nonetheless, as an unconscious way to test how firm your resolve is.

Take, for example, when a girl ignores you. Again – refer to the story I just told. The best way to deal with this test of your frame, is to give her space and not chase her.

What if she flirts with other guys in front of you? This one is a little trickier.

On the one hand, non-possessiveness is an attractive quality. On the other hand, however, being possessive and protective *after a certain period of time* can be a turn on for women.

For example, there have been times where I'm fucking a girl, and I order her to yell out: "I'm your bitch, Jon! I'm your bitch!" I'll make her say she's my little slut, and other things like that.

I'll tell her things like: "You're mine. You're my fucking property. I own you. This pussy is mine. Your body is mine. You're my fucking sex slave, and you will do as I say. Got that?"

I know it's crass, but most of the women I have sexy with enjoy it. They will start cumming almost immediately after I order them to say these things, because it excites them.

Women LOVE being objectified and possessed by an alpha male, even if they will never admit it. Every woman has a very ancient and tribal part of her brain, that WANTS to be possessed by a strong alpha male. This is one of the great paradoxes of game.

On the one hand, you don't want to become too possessive too fast. BUT, after a certain point, a certain level of possessiveness is normal, and she'll actually enjoy it.

Why? Again, think of a daddy setting boundaries for his little girl. He isn't going to let her eat junk food and party all night if he's a good father, is he? Of course not.

Likewise, when you start to set boundaries for a woman, she will instinctually recognize you as her "daddy." Again, let me give you another example:

> *A few years ago, I was dating this beautiful blonde girl who was just my type. She was absolutely stunning, and had a body to kill for. She knew how to use her feminine energy to get what she wanted, and most guys bowed down to it. I did not.*

223

One night, after we'd been hooking up for a while, she decided to pull a massive shit test on me. We had made plans to hang out, which usually entailed of us having sex and doing something fun afterward – watching a movie, going out, or whatever.

Keep in mind, I'd been dating her for a while, as well – it'd been about 3 months at this point. I had treated her very well, as I always treat the women in my life well.

Anyways, I picked her up, and brought her back to my place. Again, keep in mind that her home was 25 minutes away (she didn't have a car, because she wasn't from the country), so this was a considerable time commitment for me.

When we got to my place, she seemed very sexually unreceptive and cold. "I'm not in the mood," she said. While this is fine, and obviously a woman has a right to reject a man's advances, I didn't like how she was acting this way when we had clearly set up a date.

Then, about 30 minutes later, she told me some other guy was going to pick her up, and they were going to a party. This really set me off, because I'd spent an hour driving back and forth to pick her up, and expected to have a nice night with her.

"Are you kidding me?" I said. "You're going to make me drive an hour to pick you up, not even fuck me, and then ditch me for ANOTHER fucking guy?"

I stared her down. I could tell she was testing me. "Yes," she said, as she flipped her hair to the side in that confident manner that she always did.

"That's so fucking rude," I told her. Again, I stared her down, waiting for her to respond. She didn't say anything. She just looked away as if she didn't even care.

"You know what? Fine. Go fuck that other dude. I don't even fucking care. Go. It's fine. I'll just go fuck some other girl tonight, if you're going to treat me like that."

"He's just a friend," she said. I knew this was absolute bullshit. "Sure, yeah, okay. He's just a friend. Fine then, go hang out with your fucking friend. Go. I don't care."

Long story short, we got into a huge argument. She gave me all the typical nonsense lines like "Stop being so possessive!" and "Why do you care so much?"

I told her that I "cared so much" because it's fucking rude. "Why do you even care?" she said. "You can just go fuck any other girl."

"I know I can go fuck any other girl," I told her. "But I want to fuck YOU. If you're going to treat me like a bitch though, then I don't want to fuck you, and you can leave."

She looked me dead in the eye and said: "I want you to fuck me."

What then proceeded to happen, was some of the best, angry makeup sex that I'd ever had in my entire life. I pinned her down and ravished her, and she loved it.

She was filled with more passion and fury than I'd ever seen in a woman before, and one thing was clear: I was a man that she could not boss around or manipulate.

The average guy won't understand an exchange like this, because the average guy doesn't understand how women think.

The average guy will see a story like this, and either think it's a total lie, or go into full "white knight" mode, and call me an abusive jerk for yelling at her.

The fact of the matter is though, that setting a boundary turned her on. Being able to walk away from her turned her on. Not putting up with her bullshit turned her on.

This was the type of girl who was _drop-dead gorgeous._ I kid you not. She would turn heads wherever we'd go, and she knew the power she had over men.

Beautiful women understand the power that they have – believe me, they aren't stupid. They know that most men will literally bend over backwards and disgrace themselves if they think it'll get them a chance at even a little bit of sexual attention from her.

Of course, as I'm sure you can tell by now, this only ever backfires. If I had just told her: "Oh, you want to see your friend? Okay, yeah that's okay! I love you too, babe!" she would have lost 100% of her attraction for me, because this would have signaled that I'm okay with her walking all over me.

Instead, however, when I showed her that I wasn't willing to be treated like a chump, she became more attracted to me than she'd ever been before in her life.

Now, I want to clarify something. I'm not saying that arguments like this are necessarily "good," because they're not. But, they're a necessary part of every relationship. When a woman disrespects you, you need to make it _very clear_ that you are not okay with it.

While it's sometimes tempting to just "agree to get along" with her, it is paramount that you stand up for yourself and set strong boundaries. Do not back down under any circumstances.

I've had girls threaten to falsely accuse me of rape (no joke). Even so, I don't back down. I'm not going to be bribed, blackmailed, or extorted, for shit. I am not a coward, and I never will be.

This is just one of the MANY examples that I can give you, to show how women respond to men who have a strong sense of self-worth, and who have a very strong FRAME.

Throughout my entire interaction with this girl, I held my frame. When I first met her, I held my frame. When I started dating her more, I held my frame. When she threw that massive shit test at me, I still held my fucking frame.

This is what I mean by "holding the frame." Of course, it's fine to apologize to a woman… IF you actually feel that you did something stupid or wrong. But in general, you must NEVER apologize for being a man on your purpose, or for being a man with strong boundaries.

Let me give you one last example to really let this concept of "holding the frame" sink in. I've told this story many times before on my blog, because it's filled with wisdom.

A while ago, I met this sexy girl through my social circle, let's call her "Jackie." My game was on point, so much so that she actually asked for my number, rather than the other way around. I texted her a few days later, set up a date that night, and slept with her.

We had a great time, and she seemed to be into me. We started talking about my blog, and like many women, she initially got mad. Rather than viewing me as a teacher of men, she thought I was being "manipulative" (Google: "Jon Anthony Is Learning Game Manipulative?").

About a week later, I went to a party and ran into Jackie. Needless to say, she was pretty upset at me. "You're such a

227

player!" she shouted. "You're a sexist pig, and I can't believe I even liked you in the first place!" she yelled in my face.

It was clear that she expected me to start apologizing profusely, and to get down on my knees and beg her to forgive me. Yeah, as if I was going to do that.

"I'm not sexist," I tried to tell her, but before I could even finish my sentence, she smacked me across the face.

I walked away from her, because that was not okay. Whenever a woman physically attacks you, it's time to disengage and walk away.

Even though apologizing would have likely quelled her anger in the moment, I will never apologize for my teachings. I will never apologize for helping other men discover their masculinity, and become the best versions of themselves.

I firmly believe that what I am doing is extremely important, and is making the world a better place. Do I say stupid shit sometimes? Of course. Obviously. Who doesn't?

But I'm not going to act like a cucked little boy, spit on my dignity, and apologize for my message that's helped literally tens of thousands of men across the world.

That was my frame, and I held to it. Throughout the night, she kept shit testing me. I'd be talking with other guys, and she'd come to talk to us, and flirt with the other guys to see if it bothered me.

"Wow, you have such big triceps, Jerry! They're so much bigger than yours, Jon," she'd say. I was completely unphased and just said "Yeah, you're probably right," and kept on talking about whatever else I was talking about before.

After about 30 minutes of this, she grew fed up. Despite smacking me in the face, arguing with me, throwing a temper tantrum, flirting with other guys, and shit testing me, she could not break my frame.

She then did something to me I'll never forget. She got right in my face, grabbed my cock through my pants, and angrily spat at me: "I want you to fuck me so bad."

Of course, I didn't. Instead, I ended up fucking her friend, who was much nicer to me – and, of course, this only made Jackie even angrier and even more attracted to me.

She continued to text me, asking to hang out, for the next few weeks. She would sent me naked pictures of herself, and call me Daddy, begging me to come over. This was the effect that holding my frame had on her. It 10x'd her attraction to me.

When you *hold your frame*, women will become far more attracted to you. To be fair, some will just walk out of your life if they aren't willing to submit to you. This is fine, and you should let them do so. If a woman cannot submit to you, she is bad news, and will only cause trouble.

As a whole, however, normal, emotionally healthy women are attracted to strong, dominant men, who have a rock-solid frame that can't be broken.

Keep in mind – I've apologized many times to girls before. There have been times where I'll say something and then think about it a day later, and realize how unnecessarily mean it was to her.

In situations like that, obviously, I'm going to apologize. There's nothing wrong with apologizing if you actually mean it. But never compromise who you are for a woman, or for anyone in life.

Rule 10. Always Have A Backup Plan

Often times, when a man is dating a woman that he really likes, he has a tendency to become needy. He tends to grow too attached, too quickly, and it will turn her off.

This is why I always recommend you have a "backup plan." Whether that backup plan is simply keeping a rotation of 3-4 other women around, or if you're married, having a vague idea of how you'd ever find love again if you got divorced, it's essential you take the time to create one.

Women are attracted to abundance, as are men. When a man doesn't have a "backup", it conveys a lack of abundance. Men of abundance always have not just one, but many backups.

If a woman is dating you, and she knows that you won't be able to find another date if she cancels on you, the odds are that she won't respect your time as much as she should.

When women start to realize that no other women want you, they will naturally lose attraction for you, and slowly start to disrespect your time.

The best way to remedy this, is to simply have a backup plan. Again, your own specific backup plan will vary depending on your unique dating situation, but it's important to have one.

This is why I recommend guys "play the field" for a while, before they ever settle down with a girl. When you play the field, and get experience with many women, you develop the confidence you need to be able to walk away from her if she disrespects you.

When you play the field, and create a harem of multiple women, you not only develop a valuable skillset in dealing with women, but you also get to experience abundance.

Knowing that you've built a harem in the past, and that you can do so _in the future if need be_, is a great way to ensure you've always got a backup plan.

To show you the importance of always having a backup plan, let me paint you a picture:

> _Let's say you've been dating your girlfriend for 6 months now. You've both decided to be exclusive, and not to sleep with anyone else. At first, everything was great. She was having sex with you every day of the week, you were taking her out on incredible dates, and you were both extremely happy and fulfilled as human beings._
>
> _Then, however, over time, she begins to go cold (like many women do, as a shit test). She will refuse to have sex with you, and eventually will try to "bargain" with you (AKA if you do the dishes and clean the kitchen she'll have sex with you)._
>
> _If you know for a FACT, that you could break up with her and immediately start meeting other women, and within just a month you could have a rotation of 3-4 girls going on, would you be willing to put up with that type of crap? Of course not!_
>
> _You want a relationship where a woman WANTS to have sex with you! You want her to be sexually attracted to you. You want the passion and the fire to be there for years to come. That's what every man wants, but so few men actually GET._
>
> _So, armed with the skillset to build a harem, how would you react when she starts "rationing" out sex? You'd vocalize your concerns._

"We haven't had sex in like a week," you'll say. Of course, she will test your frame, and say something like: "So what? I don't want to have sex."

Most guys, who don't understand the "Elite Dating Secrets" that this book teaches you, would simply put up with it. But not you. You're better than that.

You'd tell her something like: "Well, that's fine. If you don't want to have sex, you have a right to do that. But maybe if you aren't attracted to me anymore, then we should consider taking a break."

Just that line alone is enough to make a woman more attracted to you. When she knows you are willing to walk, and have the BACKUP PLAN necessary to do so, she will respect you and become more attracted to you.

The fact that you're willing to walk, creates attraction. "No, I don't want to take a break!" she'll tell you. "Well, I mean, if you don't want to have sex with me, do you even think this relationship is worthwhile?" you'll ask her.

Then, it will be her who's trying to maintain the relationship (as is natural for a woman to do). She will be pleasing you, so that you don't go out and find another girl.

When women know you're a high-value man who could easily find another relationship, they will be so much more eager to please you.

Do you think if Leonardo DiCaprio dates a girl, she's giving him the "cold shoulder"? FUCK NO! Do you think that George Clooney's girlfriend says she's "not in the mood"? Of course not.

Girls that date high-quality men know how important it is to please them – and when you always have a backup plan, or an escape plan, you become that high-quality man.

Now, I know what you're thinking:

> *"But Jon, isn't it manipulative to always be thinking about how you would leave her? Shouldn't you enjoy your time with her and cherish her? It seems really dysfunctional to always keep one eye on her, and one eye on a backup plan, doesn't it?"*

First off, I'd like to say that you shouldn't always be thinking about your backup plan. It's not meant to be at the forefront of your mind. It's intended as a last resort, if the relationship fails.

Second, you absolutely should enjoy your time with your girlfriend. Here's the thing, though – being able to walk away from her, ensures that you're with her because you WANT TO BE with her, not because you can't find another girl.

When you have a "backup plan" (AKA you know how to get laid and pick up chicks), it ensures that you will never get trapped into a dysfunctional relationship because you can't find another.

The goal of a backup plan isn't actually to default from your relationships – on the contrary. It's meant to ensure you never get trapped in a dysfunctional relationship, because you will always have a way to meet, attract, and seduce beautiful women.

Final Thoughts

"This is your life, and it's ending one minute at a time.

-Chuck Palahniuk, *Fight Club*

"Everything you've ever wanted is on the other side of fear."

-George Addair

I'm sure your mind is racing with thoughts right now:

- *"How do I start applying the information in this book?*
- *"Where do I even begin?"*
- *"Should I break up with my girlfriend or not?*
- *"I've failed so many of women's tests and didn't even know it!"*

This is normal. As you start to integrate the advice from this book into your life, you will notice a significant shift in your relationships.

Women will be more eager to see you. Men will be keener to be your friend. People will as a whole, respond more favorably to you – especially beautiful women.

I recommend that you read this book *AT LEAST* five times. Ideally, you should read, and re-read it 10-15 times to ensure that these concepts fully sink into your subconscious mind.

It will take time for this book to change your life. Of course, it doesn't have to take that long if you start applying its wisdom and information today.

All in all, you have an incredible journey ahead of you. Believe me, 10 years ago, I had no idea that I'd be dating and sleeping with the woman of my dreams. Yet, here I am.

Count yourself lucky, as one of the few men who has stumbled upon this book. Most of these dating secrets stay hidden from the majority of men.

In fact, it's only the elite – the top 1% of men – that knows about these things. So, give yourself a big pat on the back and congratulate yourself, my friend. You're in the top 1%.

If you have any questions, feedback, or just want to chat and ask me a question, you can feel free to reach out to me via my email: jon@masculinedevelopment.com

In addition to this, I also urge you to read my blog and subscribe to my YouTube channel. I have literally hundreds of free articles and videos, that you can peruse on your own time.

If you would like to take your life to the next level and receive access to my premium content, you can check out some of the services and products I offer below:

This was the first eBook that I ever wrote, and it's been my best-selling one ever since. It's great for guys who are overwhelmed with information, and who want a simple, proven system to 10x their confidence, dominance, and masculinity.

It also comes with 4 free bonuses (for now, I don't know if I'll take them down at some point or not):

- The Art of Tinder
- Getting Nudes Guide
- Mindset Mastery
- Night Game Domination

If you enjoyed this eBook, I can almost guarantee that you'll enjoy my 7 Strategies program.

Go to GetSevenStrategies.com to learn more!

This was the second eBook that I launched, and is primarily focused on teaching you how to develop the "alpha male physique" that I mentioned in this book.

Like all my products, this one also comes with a bunch of free bonuses, on me:

- Exercise Demonstration Guide
- Alpha Supplements
- Pumped to Pull Fitness Game Guide

Tons of dudes have transformed their bodies using this program, and it covers everything from my own personal workout routine, to the supplements I use, and even how to design your own nutrition plan based on your needs.

Go to GetThePerfectBody.com to learn more!

In case you can't tell, I'm a pretty outspoken guy. I don't like dealing with the bullshit office politics in most corporate jobs, and I hate being bossed around by stuck up bureaucrats who control my salary.

If you can relate to this, consider checking out my course on trading cryptocurrencies. It's helped countless men quit their jobs and make a 6-figure income from home, so they can abandon the toxic corporate workplace once and for all.

Like all my products, it comes with bonuses:

- Full Access to My Trades, with 24/7 Alerts
- Regular Market Updates
- Invitation to Join Our Exclusive Insider's Group

With the tumultuous markets of crypto, there's money to be made all the time.

Go to GetBitcoinMillionaire.com to learn more!

Final Thoughts

Again, I urge you to read, and re-read this book 10-15 times over, so that it can fully sink into your subconscious. As you go out into the dating world, you'll find yourself making many of the same mistakes which I address in this book, without even realizing it.

If you enjoyed this book, please consider giving me a 5-Star Review on Amazon. I am entirely self-employed and have dedicated my life to helping men across the world unlock their true potential as alpha males, so your support is much appreciated.

All in all, I wish you the best of luck on your dating journey. I know it may sound strange to say this, because I've never met you, but in some sense, I feel that we share a deep connection.

In some sense, you were probably like me a few years ago – upset, discontent, and dissatisfied with your current dating life. If this is you, I can relate.

I remember what it was like to feel hopeless, anxious, and depressed all the time. I know what it's like to hate your dating life, and to feel completely lost when it comes to understanding, attracting, and seducing women.

Believe me, my friend... you have no clue how good things will get. Over the next few months, as you begin to apply the concepts discussed within this book, your eyes will grow wide with shock and awe, as you see your life transform before your very eyes.

I always love hearing from my readers, so if you would like to submit a success story, ask a question, or again, just talk, you email me here: jon@masculinedevelopment.com

As always, I hope you enjoyed the content that I wrote. I hope you gained more from it than you ever thought possible, and from my heart to yours, I wish you the best and will see you next time.

To Your Success,

Jon Anthony